Advanced ZBrush Handbook

Master Sculpting, Detailing, and Innovation for the Modern Artist

STEVEN S. BELLS

TABLE OF CONTENTS

Preface

Sculpting in the digital space has undergone a profound transformation. What began as simple polygonal modeling has matured into complex workflows capable of producing forms that rival the intricacy of traditional clay sculpture. ZBrush, a program originally designed as a tool for painting in 2.5D, evolved into a revolutionary platform that redefined how artists approach digital creation.

This handbook was born from the pressing need for an updated, truly advanced resource. Many artists today find themselves stuck at an intermediate level—comfortable with basic techniques, yet unable to push their skills into the domain of high-end professional work. Tutorials often rehash the same beginner content, leaving a significant gap for those who aspire to produce museum-quality sculpts, cinematic assets, or cutting-edge game models.

The **Advanced ZBrush Handbook** is crafted to close that gap. It moves beyond elementary techniques and dives into professional methodologies that are used in high-pressure environments such as film, game development, 3D printing, and fine art. The emphasis is placed on control, precision, innovation, and workflow efficiency. It teaches not just what buttons to press, but why certain approaches yield superior results.

Rather than chasing trends or novelty features, this handbook distills practical strategies and insights gained from years of hands-on experience with the software. Each chapter is designed to help the reader refine their sculpting intuition, develop independent problem-solving skills, and work faster without sacrificing quality.

The goal is simple: to raise the technical and artistic ceiling for serious ZBrush users and to encourage a level of mastery that makes digital sculpture indistinguishable from handcrafted art.

This book is more than a collection of tricks. It is a blueprint for those who aim to produce work that commands respect in professional studios, freelance platforms, and personal exhibitions. Whether your goal is artistic expression or technical excellence, the following chapters are structured to serve as your guide.

The Evolution of ZBrush and Why This Book Exists

When ZBrush first appeared in the early 2000s, it was seen as an oddity. Traditional 3D artists, accustomed to rigid modeling software, often dismissed it as a novelty. Yet under its unconventional surface lay an entirely new philosophy of creation—one centered around the freedom to sculpt digitally with the same immediacy and tactility as physical mediums.

As years progressed, ZBrush introduced features like ZSpheres, Dynamesh, ZRemesher, and Live Boolean operations—each release peeling away limitations that once constrained digital sculptors. Techniques that once required laborious topology management and meticulous vertex pushing could now be achieved intuitively. Artists were freed to focus on form, detail, and expression rather than technical barriers.

In the last few years, ZBrush has seen even more rapid development. Dynamic systems such as Sculptris Pro, enhanced rendering capabilities, improved performance handling of high-polygon models, and expanded plugin support have expanded its reach into industries ranging from feature films to fine art installations. It has become the de facto standard for character sculpting, concept modeling, collectibles, prosthetics design, and even experimental architecture.

Yet despite the incredible power now packed into the program, many artists still approach it using outdated methods or incomplete workflows. Tutorials often focus heavily on isolated features without teaching the underlying thought processes that unlock the software's full capabilities.

This book exists because advanced ZBrush knowledge is not simply about learning more features—it is about **elevating your entire approach**. It is about understanding the software deeply enough to bend it to your artistic will, rather than being led by it.

Too many resources offer recipes without teaching the skills necessary to invent your own. This handbook is structured differently. It assumes the reader is ready to move beyond memorization and into mastery. Here, you will learn not only techniques but advanced workflows, decision-making processes, troubleshooting methods, and the small professional habits that separate seasoned artists from hobbyists.

The need for such a resource is more urgent now than ever. As digital sculpting becomes increasingly competitive and sophisticated, standing still means falling behind. The Advanced ZBrush Handbook aims to equip you with the tools, insights, and mindset necessary to stay ahead.

Who This Handbook Is For

This handbook is not for beginners. It does not teach basic navigation, simple brush settings, or the foundational aspects of sculpting that are already widely covered elsewhere. Instead, it assumes the reader has an operational familiarity with ZBrush and a strong desire to advance far beyond the fundamentals.

It is written for digital artists who are already creating but are unsatisfied with the plateau they have reached. It serves sculptors who want to move from intermediate work to professional-quality models that can stand alongside those seen in film productions, game development studios, collectible manufacturing, and fine art galleries.

Character artists who seek more believable anatomy, hard surface modelers who need cleaner mechanical designs, texture artists aiming for richer surface detailing, and concept artists who want to prototype ideas faster—all will find practical value in these pages.

Freelancers will benefit from workflow efficiencies and presentation techniques that attract better-paying clients. Students and educators can use the insights here to raise the technical standards of their portfolios and programs. Even seasoned professionals will find advanced tips and unconventional workflows that sharpen their competitive edge.

More importantly, this handbook is for those willing to challenge their current habits. Mastery requires more than passive consumption of knowledge; it demands the active reshaping of one's approach to both software and artistry. Readers who engage with the techniques and exercises here will not only sculpt better—they will think differently about how they sculpt.

If you are content with surface-level knowledge, this handbook is not for you. But if you are committed to achieving mastery, to pushing the boundaries of your skill, and to producing work that speaks without needing explanation, then you will find what you are looking for within these chapters.

Sculpting Beyond Limits

Rethinking Forms: Advanced Mesh Blocking Strategies

Every great sculpture, whether digital or traditional, begins with a strong foundation. Yet, many artists fall into the trap of rushing into details without establishing robust underlying forms. True mastery starts with learning how to block intelligently. Advanced mesh blocking in ZBrush requires more than simply shaping primitives—it demands strategic thinking about structure, weight distribution, and gesture from the earliest stages.

Instead of relying on a single sphere or cube to build an entire figure, seasoned artists often break down their concepts into multiple, manageable sections. Each major mass—head, torso, pelvis, limbs—is blocked independently, respecting anatomical rhythm and balance. Using multiple subtools or carefully merged shapes allows for greater control and flexibility during early development.

Dynamesh remains a key ally during this phase, but rather than using it indiscriminately, professionals remesh only at critical points. Frequent Dynameshing can collapse intentional forms, so a measured approach is essential. A sculptor might initially block in using very low-resolution Dynamesh settings to establish gesture, then selectively remesh higher when surface transitions and muscle groups are in place.

ZSpheres are another tool often overlooked in favor of quicker methods, yet their value is unmatched when designing figures with complex poses. Creating an accurate skeletal structure with ZSpheres first ensures that proportions and anatomy remain grounded even as surface complexity grows. Professionals leverage ZSphere armatures to block in not just organic forms but also hard surface concepts, robotic limbs, and dynamic armor configurations.

Thinking in terms of modularity during blocking also pays dividends later. Instead of treating the figure as a single monolithic object, successful sculpts are often conceived as layered systems: underlying skeleton, muscle masses, secondary elements like cloth or armor, and tertiary details like accessories. Each layer is thought through independently before they merge into a seamless final work.

Advanced mesh blocking, therefore, is less about speed and more about strategic thinking. Time spent creating intelligent base structures shortens the detailing phase dramatically and leads to sculptures that feel intentional rather than chaotic.

Dynamic Forms vs Traditional Sculpting

Traditional sculpting methods, even when transposed to digital platforms, often emphasize building forms slowly through additive and subtractive processes. This workflow values deliberate construction but can sometimes restrict spontaneity and limit the artist's ability to respond fluidly to creative instincts.

Dynamic sculpting techniques, by contrast, embrace flexibility from the beginning. Digital sculptors today leverage tools like Sculptris Pro and Dynamesh to reshape their models continuously, treating digital clay as something truly malleable rather than rigid. Instead of setting permanent structural decisions early, dynamic sculpting encourages ongoing refinement and adaptation.

One of the greatest advantages of dynamic forms is the freedom it gives artists to prioritize gesture and emotional expression. By focusing first on the flow of mass and movement, without worrying about technical topology constraints, sculptors can capture energy that might otherwise be lost. Loose, energetic early forms are gradually tightened and refined, allowing the artwork to evolve organically.

However, dynamic sculpting is not an excuse for chaos. Without a solid understanding of anatomy, structure, and proportion, dynamic workflows can lead to unstable models that collapse under their own inconsistencies. Therefore, an advanced artist balances freedom with discipline—sculpting dynamically but checking constantly against reference and structural knowledge.

Knowing when to shift between dynamic and traditional methods is also critical. Some phases of a sculpt benefit from the freeform creativity of dynamic workflows, while others—such as precise facial modeling, mechanical components, or tight clothing folds—require more methodical and traditional techniques. Mastering both approaches and moving fluidly between them as needed distinguishes advanced sculptors from intermediate ones.

Customizing Brushes for Sculpting Efficiency

Efficiency in ZBrush is not merely about using the right brushes but about **adapting brushes to suit the way you think and sculpt**. Default brush settings serve as a starting point, but true professionals fine-tune brushes to match their personal style and project requirements.

Customizing a brush can involve multiple adjustments. Modifying the curve graph, adjusting falloff, tweaking the alpha, and changing stroke settings all dramatically affect how a brush behaves. A Clay Buildup brush, for example, can be softened to behave more like wet clay, perfect for early block-ins. A Standard brush can be reshaped into a sharper tool ideal for cutting crisp folds into fabric or muscle striations into anatomy.

Creating specialized brushes for specific tasks not only speeds up workflows but also ensures consistency across a model. Having a dedicated brush for defining primary forms, a different one for secondary surface undulations, and another for micro detailing allows an artist to layer complexity logically without having to constantly recalibrate tools mid-session.

In addition to brush customization, assigning hotkeys and grouping brushes into logical folders saves countless hours over the life of a project. Custom UI arrangements that bring essential brushes to the forefront prevent unnecessary interruptions to creative flow.

Advanced sculptors even develop entire brush sets tailored to specific projects. For example, a creature design project might demand brushes that simulate organic bone textures, torn flesh, and chitinous surfaces, while a hard surface modeling project might require beveling, panel cutting, and trim detailing brushes.

Ultimately, brush customization is not about making ZBrush behave differently—it is about making it behave **as an extension of your hand**. When brushes are tuned properly, they feel invisible, allowing focus to remain entirely on the sculpture itself rather than the interface.

Secrets of Effective Silhouette Control

A weak silhouette signals an unfinished or poorly conceived sculpture, no matter how much internal detail it holds. In both two-dimensional and three-dimensional art, the silhouette—the outermost shape of a form—is a primary tool for communicating strength, readability, and character.

Effective silhouette control begins during the earliest blocking phases. Rather than focusing on interior details, the sculptor first ensures that the overall outer shape reads clearly from multiple angles. A figure, creature, or object must have a distinct and recognizable contour before any internal forms are polished.

In ZBrush, frequent use of the Flat Color material and turning models into pure black or white helps strip away distractions caused by lighting and shading. Viewing sculpts in flat silhouette mode allows artists to check the strength of their contours objectively. Areas that feel muddy, noisy, or overly complicated can then be reworked into cleaner, more purposeful lines.

Contrary to what some may believe, effective silhouettes are not about making outlines symmetrical or overly smooth. The best silhouettes often feature controlled asymmetry, unexpected angles, and varied rhythms of negative space. These elements create visual interest and keep the viewer's eye moving naturally around the figure.

Sharp corners, intentional breaks in rhythm, and strong gesture lines are tools used by expert sculptors to inject energy into silhouettes. Small tweaks to the angle of an arm, the curve of a hip, or the tilt of a helmet can dramatically improve the sculpture's visual impact.

Furthermore, silhouette thinking does not end once detailing begins. Every secondary and tertiary form must respect and enhance the silhouette rather than break it down. Ornamental details, armor plating, or muscle striations should reinforce the character of the outer contour, not fight against it.

Professional digital sculptors develop a habit of squinting at their work, zooming out frequently, and using silhouette checks as part of their normal workflow—not just at the beginning, but continuously throughout the sculpting process.

By mastering silhouette control, artists ensure their work commands attention even from across the room—or, in the digital age, across a crowded portfolio screen.

Mastering Dynamesh, ZRemesher, and Sculptris Pro

Deep Optimization of Dynamesh for Complex Surfaces

Dynamesh remains one of the most transformative tools available for digital sculptors. At its essence, Dynamesh allows artists to remesh their models uniformly without concern for underlying topology, promoting uninterrupted creativity. However, using Dynamesh skillfully requires more than simply activating it and sculpting at random.

Advanced Dynamesh optimization begins with understanding resolution management. Setting an appropriate Dynamesh resolution is not about guessing or following arbitrary numbers. The scale of the model dictates how much detail Dynamesh can capture. Larger models require higher resolution values to maintain surface sharpness, while smaller models can work effectively with lower values. Therefore, it becomes critical to first set the model's size appropriately before initiating Dynamesh, often using the 'Unify' option temporarily for calibration.

When working with complex surfaces—such as multi-limbed creatures, intricate armor pieces, or layered fabrics—there is a risk of losing form integrity during remeshing. To counter this, professionals often isolate major parts into separate subtools before Dynameshing. This prevents small overlapping components from fusing improperly and maintains cleaner mass separation.

Polish settings within Dynamesh also deserve careful adjustment. By default, smoothing can erode important sculpted features. Experienced users often disable polish during early Dynamesh passes and selectively re-enable it when transitioning to refinement stages. This strategy ensures that vital volumes and planar transitions are preserved while still benefiting from topology cleaning.

Another advanced tactic involves the use of inserted meshes and booleans with Dynamesh. Rather than hand-sculpting complex mechanical forms, artists insert simple meshes (like cylinders, spheres, or custom shapes), position them, and then perform a controlled Dynamesh remesh. The inserted pieces are merged seamlessly, allowing for faster construction of hard surface and hybrid designs without compromising surface complexity.

Dynamesh is not merely a tool for beginners seeking forgiveness from topology errors. In professional hands, it becomes a precision instrument for creating dense, highly dynamic, and readable forms that would be arduous to manage through manual retopology at early stages.

When (and When Not) to Use Sculptris Pro

Sculptris Pro mode offers a dynamic tessellation system, allowing sculptors to add fine details without worrying about stretching or crushing topology. Every stroke automatically adjusts the density of polygons beneath the brush, which means surface complexity grows exactly where needed and remains light elsewhere. This behavior can significantly accelerate creativity, especially during early concept phases.

However, knowing when to employ Sculptris Pro—and when to avoid it—is critical for producing professional-quality work.

Sculptris Pro excels in areas that demand organic complexity. Creating wrinkled skin textures, intricate creature details, fine scars, ornamental carvings, and rocky surfaces all benefit from Sculptris Pro's localized tessellation. The artist can sketch complex ideas without being trapped by technical restrictions, allowing forms to evolve naturally as needed.

Despite these strengths, Sculptris Pro introduces challenges when it comes to managing structural consistency. Since it generates dense geometry in isolated areas, models sculpted extensively in Sculptris Pro can develop uneven polygon distribution. This irregularity creates problems later during subdivision, polishing, or retopology, particularly when sharp mechanical edges or smooth surfaces are required.

Another risk arises when switching between Sculptris Pro and traditional subdivision workflows. Models tessellated unevenly cannot be subdivided cleanly without causing distortions. Therefore, artists working on projects that require clean production-ready topology should view Sculptris Pro as a temporary phase tool rather than a permanent solution.

Advanced sculptors often use Sculptris Pro selectively. It may be activated briefly to establish secondary and tertiary details on localized parts of a mesh and then turned off once the intended refinement is achieved. Following these adjustments, a ZRemesher pass or manual retopology ensures that the project remains manageable and professional.

Sculptris Pro serves as a bridge between pure creativity and technical discipline. Using it responsibly ensures it strengthens, rather than undermines, the sculpting process.

ZRemesher Tricks for Clean Mechanical and Organic Meshes

ZRemesher has evolved far beyond its early incarnations, offering remarkable control over the topology of both organic forms and mechanical objects. Still, achieving truly clean results demands a strategic approach rather than a reliance on default settings.

One fundamental step is setting up proper ZRemesher Guides. These guides allow artists to sketch flow directions manually across their model, encouraging ZRemesher to follow natural muscle loops, facial edge loops, or hard surface seams. Spending a few minutes drawing smart guide curves saves hours of corrective work later.

For organic sculpts, balancing adaptive size settings is essential. Lowering adaptive size values leads to more uniform topology, which benefits high-detail areas such as faces and hands. Higher adaptive size settings allow larger polygons to occupy less important areas, such as flat torsos or backs. Adjusting this balance prevents unnecessary polygon overcrowding where it is not needed, improving both performance and sculpting clarity.

When working with mechanical shapes, maintaining edge sharpness becomes the primary challenge. Hard surface models often suffer from excessive rounding and loss of structural clarity after automatic remeshing. To solve this, advanced users employ the following techniques:

- **Edge Masking Before ZRemesh:** Masking critical edges and creases forces ZRemesher to preserve these zones during remeshing.

- **Crease Edge Tagging:** Using the 'Crease' function combined with Keep Creases activated during ZRemeshing helps maintain sharp transitions.

- **Polygroups Control:** Dividing surfaces into intelligent polygroups based on material changes or form breaks gives ZRemesher clear instructions on where to separate flows.

For particularly complex mechanical assets, an effective method involves temporarily slicing the mesh into multiple grouped pieces using the Slice Curve brush, ZRemeshing them individually with polygroups intact, and then merging them back together after remeshing is complete. This modular approach enables higher control over difficult surfaces that resist single-pass cleanups.

In both organic and mechanical workflows, using the ZRemesher Half option iteratively produces superior results compared to forcing low polygon counts in one pass. Shrinking the mesh gradually allows the algorithm to resolve complex flow transitions more accurately.

Ultimately, successful ZRemeshing is not about pushing a button and accepting the output. It is an interactive process where the artist guides the tool thoughtfully, resulting in meshes that are not only technically sound but also visually beautiful and structurally intelligent.

Surface Detailing on a Microscopic Level

Micro-Mesh Texturing Techniques

Surface detailing has evolved from simple bump mapping into a complex discipline requiring a deep understanding of physical texture representation. Micro-mesh texturing stands as one of the most potent techniques for introducing believable surface complexity without compromising sculptural integrity.

At its foundation, micro-mesh texturing involves applying tiny, repeating structures across a model's surface. These micro-details can represent anything from cloth weaves, fine scales, skin pores, chipped paint, to weathered stone erosion. Unlike traditional displacement methods, micro-mesh techniques integrate physical geometry onto the surface, allowing for actual sculptural interactions with light and shadow rather than simulated depth alone.

A sophisticated approach to micro-mesh usage requires careful preparation of the base surface. A clean, evenly subdivided surface prevents distortion when applying micro-details. Before introducing micro-mesh patterns, artists typically ensure that the model holds enough polygon density to accommodate high-frequency information. Without sufficient geometry, micro-patterns appear stretched, broken, or muddy.

When preparing custom micro-meshes, artists often sculpt or model small tileable patterns separately. These tiles are then converted into brushes or imported as nano-mesh inserts, depending on the desired control level. Critical to success is ensuring seamless tiling and maintaining uniform scale. Small mistakes at the tiling stage compound significantly when distributed over large areas.

Selective application of micro-mesh textures prevents visual overload. High-frequency details should enhance focal points—such as facial zones, contact edges on armor, or exposed surfaces of worn tools—while less critical areas can be treated more subtly. This controlled application draws the viewer's eye intelligently across the piece, enhancing realism without creating a chaotic or noisy surface.

Mastery of micro-mesh texturing requires understanding that not every surface demands detail saturation. Professional sculptors know that strategic emptiness often strengthens the impact of detailed zones.

Layer-Based Detailing Workflows

Layer-based workflows offer artists a non-destructive method for managing and refining surface details. By isolating different levels of detail into individual layers, sculptors can adjust, blend, or eliminate elements freely without risking the underlying form.

At the technical level, layering is more than simple organizational convenience. Layers can record brush strokes, intensity values, and deformation amounts separately, giving the artist surgical control over the model's evolution. For instance, subtle secondary wrinkles can be intensified temporarily to judge their visual impact before committing. If they clash with tertiary pore structures later, their opacity can be reduced or their influence blended back seamlessly.

When building layer-based workflows, professionals follow a structured approach. Base forms are established on the primary mesh without active layers to ensure solidity. Once satisfied, the sculptor creates a new layer specifically for secondary forms—bony landmarks, major wrinkles, and muscular separations. Tertiary details like fine wrinkles, pores, and micro-scars are reserved for additional layers stacked above.

One powerful method involves creating experimental layers dedicated solely to alternative texture treatments. A surface might have a cracked dry mud effect in one layer and a smooth polished version in another. By toggling these layers, the artist can preview variations without reworking the base model.

For maximum control, each layer's intensity should be kept subtle during creation. Overdriven details tend to clash later when compounded with other fine structures. Subtle layering preserves naturalistic detail buildup and avoids the common pitfall of over-sculpting.

Proper layer naming conventions, while often overlooked, significantly improve efficiency during complex projects. Clear labels such as "Primary Wrinkles," "Secondary Skin Folds," or "Surface Imperfections" prevent confusion during later revision stages, especially when collaborating with teams.

A disciplined layer-based workflow transforms sculpting from an irreversible process into a flexible creative dialogue between form and detail.

Advanced Use of Alphas and Custom Alpha Creation

Alphas—black and white images representing height information—serve as one of the most versatile tools in a sculptor's arsenal. They allow intricate details to be stamped, dragged, or masked onto a model's surface, generating complex textures that would be laborious to sculpt manually.

While pre-made alpha libraries offer a wide range of choices, relying exclusively on generic sources risks creating uninspired or derivative work. Custom alpha creation elevates a sculptor's work by introducing unique patterns tailored precisely to a project's needs.

To create effective custom alphas, an artist begins by understanding the target surface characteristics. Skin pores, for instance, require chaotic, irregular patterns, while fabric weaves demand ordered, repetitive structures. Artists can generate alphas by hand-painting grayscale images in external software, photographing real-world surfaces and converting them to high-contrast formats, or sculpting high-resolution tiles and exporting height maps.

Resolution matters tremendously. Low-resolution alphas blur fine details, undermining the intended texture sharpness. Conversely, extremely high-resolution alphas inflate file sizes unnecessarily and can slow sculpting responsiveness. A balance must be struck, with typical professional alphas ranging between 2K to 4K resolution, depending on project scale.

Control during alpha application is equally important. Advanced brush settings such as roll rate, focal shift, and stroke spacing allow the sculptor to blend alphas naturally onto surfaces. Instead of obvious stamp marks, well-applied alphas integrate fluidly, suggesting complexity without revealing the tool's mechanical origin.

When layering alphas, restraint and planning are essential. Overlapping radically different alphas without thought can create surface noise that reads as unintentional damage rather than purposeful texture. Professionals map out alpha application zones in advance, often masking specific areas to receive particular alpha treatments, ensuring coherence across the model.

Alpha usage is most powerful when seen not as a shortcut but as an extension of the sculptor's vision, providing an intricate vocabulary to articulate surface language with precision.

True-to-Life Pore and Wrinkle Sculpting

True realism in character and creature sculpting lives or dies on the credibility of pores and wrinkles. These microstructures communicate an enormous amount about age, ethnicity, lifestyle, material type, and surface condition.

Achieving authentic pore and wrinkle work requires far more than spamming noise generators or dragging alpha stamps. First and foremost, understanding anatomical behavior is vital. Wrinkles follow specific mechanical laws—compression folds perpendicular to stress, stretching folds aligned with tension. For example, crow's feet radiate from the eye corners outward, following the orbital muscle's contraction patterns. Forehead wrinkles generally run horizontally, responding to brow elevation.

Pores, conversely, appear distributed unevenly across the skin, clustering in oilier regions like the nose, forehead, and chin. Different body zones feature different pore densities and sizes; a pore-heavy shoulder texture differs significantly from the smoother skin of the underarm.

Professionals approach pore and wrinkle sculpting hierarchically:

1. **Macro Wrinkles:** These include major expression folds like nasolabial lines or forehead creases, sculpted with standard brushes at medium subdivision levels.

2. **Secondary Wrinkles:** Smaller folds intersecting macro wrinkles are added next, creating realistic layering and reinforcing natural skin stretching.

3. **Tertiary Details:** Fine wrinkles and pores are applied at the highest subdivision levels using custom brushes, noise modifiers, or hand-sculpted strokes.

A critical yet often missed step is micro-breakup. In reality, even freshly hydrated skin is not perfectly smooth. Tiny surface irregularities catch highlights and add believability. Gentle noise application, combined with pore detailing, adds this final layer of realism.

Moreover, pore and wrinkle sharpness must be managed carefully. Over-sharpened features read as stylized or aged artificially. A professional trick involves lightly smoothing pore and wrinkle sculpting passes to soften transitions, matching the more organic, less mechanical look of actual skin.

Sculpting pores and wrinkles is less about copying textures and more about interpreting the physical behavior of material under motion, age, and environment.

Hard Surface Sculpting: Precision Engineering

Redefining Hard Surface Workflows in ZBrush

Hard surface sculpting once carried a reputation for being tedious and technically limiting within traditional digital sculpting tools. However, through refined workflows and methodical techniques, ZBrush has shifted from being a purely organic sculpting environment to a precision platform capable of producing complex mechanical forms with extraordinary accuracy.

Modern hard surface workflows prioritize control over every aspect of form generation. Rather than trying to force organic tools to produce rigid structures, professionals now use hybrid workflows that blend sculpting freedom with calculated construction. This balance allows artists to block out basic volumes quickly, yet achieve the crispness and mechanical believability expected from industrial designs, robotics, armor, weapons, and mechanical props.

Key to redefining hard surface efficiency is understanding how to sculpt non-destructively. Early mistakes often stem from merging too many forms too soon or working destructively without planning. Instead, contemporary workflows advocate treating each component independently until final assembly, allowing detailed refinement without compromising surrounding structures.

Another breakthrough is the emphasis on subdivision hierarchy management. By maintaining low subdivision levels for broad shape control and reserving higher levels for surface refinements, artists prevent form collapse and maintain the ability to adjust proportions throughout the build.

Symmetry use is also strategic rather than automatic. While early block-outs benefit from symmetry, asymmetrical elements—damage, wear, design offsets—are introduced intentionally at later stages to avoid an artificial, mirrored look.

Ultimately, modern hard surface workflows in ZBrush demand a mentality shift: from freeform organic expression to calculated, engineered construction, where every cutline, panel, and contour serves both functional and aesthetic purposes.

Panel Loops, Booleans, and Live Boolean Mastery

Three powerhouse techniques stand as pillars for serious hard surface work: **Panel Loops**, **Booleans**, and **Live Booleans**. Each method offers a specific form of control over surface division, mechanical design, and volume subtraction or addition.

Panel Loops allow artists to transform simple surfaces into multi-layered structures, simulating plating, armor seams, or modular constructions without heavy manual labor. Correct use of Panel Loops depends heavily on clean polygrouping beforehand. When each surface section is isolated by color-coded polygroups, Panel Loops can extrude, bevel, and polish each segment independently, creating perfect separations and edge transitions that mimic manufactured assembly.

Booleans, especially when mastered through **Live Boolean**, change the way artists think about object creation entirely. Instead of modeling a form directly, sculptors construct a "negative space" workflow: combining additive and subtractive shapes live, visualizing the final outcome in real-time without committing destructive actions until satisfied.

Effective use of Live Boolean demands an understanding of object hierarchy and visibility. Subtools can be flagged to add, subtract, or intersect with each other dynamically. This allows experimentation without fear, as modifications remain live and reversible up to the moment of baking the result into true geometry.

Critical to Boolean success is preparation. Meshes intended for Boolean operations must be watertight, with no hidden double faces or non-manifold edges. Sloppy source meshes often produce baking errors, ruining edge clarity and creating cleanup nightmares.

After baking Booleans, most professionals immediately retopologize or clean the resulting geometry. Booleans tend to create unnecessarily dense or messy topology, which, if left unchecked, can cause issues in later detailing, UV mapping, or rendering stages.

Together, mastery over Panel Loops and Boolean systems grants artists the ability to engineer intricate hard surface models with mechanical authenticity, reducing sculpting bottlenecks and massively improving productivity.

Nailing Edge Precision and Maintaining Form Integrity

Hard surface models are judged by the discipline of their edges and the consistency of their volumes. A model riddled with uneven bevels, warping surfaces, or wobbly contours instantly breaks immersion and exposes technical weaknesses.

Nailing edge precision requires more than just clean strokes—it demands careful planning of where edges are introduced, how they transition, and what purpose they serve. In manufactured objects, edges are rarely random; they manage stress distribution, visual breakups, and user safety.

In digital sculpting, achieving perfect edge control means developing an intimate relationship with your brush settings, subdivision handling, and masking techniques.

Sculptors working at too high of a subdivision level too early often struggle to control their edges. To maintain form integrity, artists rough out blocky, simple shapes at low resolution, concentrating on proportion and silhouette first. Sharpening of edges happens gradually, stepping up subdivision only when absolutely necessary.

The **TrimDynamic**, **hPolish**, and **ClipCurve** brushes have become essential allies in achieving mechanical crispness. Used correctly, these brushes help flatten surfaces, sharpen transitions, and maintain planar consistency. When these tools are combined with masking and deformations like Inflate or Polish by Features, hard edges can be tuned with remarkable subtlety.

Form integrity is preserved by avoiding unnecessary distortions. Many mistakes occur when artists over-manipulate subdivisions, causing unintended stretching. A disciplined artist resets forms constantly, smoothing while preserving structure, rather than letting surface noise accumulate unchecked.

Moreover, careful attention to silhouette review ensures that hard surface designs remain visually strong from every angle. Checking models under multiple lighting conditions and viewing angles during the sculpting process helps catch and correct minor deformations that may not be obvious under default settings.

Ultimately, true edge mastery comes from patience, control, and a deliberate workflow—where every surface and line is placed with intent, not by accident.

Kitbashing for Advanced Users

Kitbashing, when practiced at a professional level, elevates production speed and detail quality while maintaining creative flexibility. It involves assembling complex models by combining pre-made mechanical components—known as kits—into new designs.

While beginners often treat kitbashing as little more than piling pieces randomly, seasoned artists apply strict design logic. Good kitbashing preserves functional believability: mechanical parts appear engineered for a reason, fitting into designs in a way that suggests purpose rather than chaotic assembly.

Advanced users approach kitbashing with a library of custom-built or commercially available parts, ranging from simple bolts and pistons to full modular panels and hinge systems. These libraries are meticulously curated and often expanded over years of professional work.

The key to successful advanced kitbashing lies in three critical practices:

1. **Scale Consistency:** All parts must exist in the same believable scale. An oversized bolt on a delicate wrist assembly instantly destroys realism.

2. **Design Cohesion:** Kits should share design language—matching bevel widths, surface treatments, and material assumptions—to avoid clashing visual styles.

3. **Purposeful Placement:** Each added part should serve an implied mechanical function. Hinges should suggest movement, vents should imply cooling, and fasteners should indicate assembly points.

In ZBrush, kitbashing efficiency is boosted through the InsertMesh and NanoMesh systems. InsertMesh allows instant insertion of prebuilt components along surface curves, while NanoMesh supports procedural repetition of components across surfaces with fine control over size, angle, and distribution.

Despite the advantages, professionals avoid leaning on kitbashing as a crutch. Overuse or careless deployment results in generic, cluttered designs lacking originality. True mastery uses kitbash elements as foundations or accents, but the unique form and silhouette of the piece must always dominate.

Advanced kitbashing is not about shortcutting creativity but about amplifying it—speeding up construction without sacrificing vision or craftsmanship.

Complex Anatomy and Creature Design

Building Anatomically Correct Models from Scratch

Sculpting anatomically correct figures requires more than a surface-level understanding of form; it demands a disciplined process rooted in structure, proportion, and purpose. When building a model from scratch, the foundation lies not in detailing but in establishing a believable skeletal framework first.

The process begins with constructing the basic skeletal structure, which defines proportions, posture, and overall silhouette. In digital sculpting, this often takes the form of a simple blockout using primitive shapes, each representing major bones: skull, ribcage, pelvis, femur, humerus, and spine. Instead of fixating on details too early, the focus remains on correctly spacing and scaling these components relative to each other.

Only after the skeleton is proportionally sound do muscles enter the conversation. Musculature should be applied in layers, reflecting their real-world origins, insertions, and overlaps. Attention to the natural tension and relaxation of muscles based on pose ensures the figure maintains believability even before surface refinement.

Artists aiming for accuracy must study not just anatomy books, but dynamic references—athletes in motion, medical imaging, and anatomical sculptures—allowing them to see how body systems interact under real-world stresses.

Building models from scratch also demands a commitment to revisiting and adjusting earlier decisions. Early-stage anatomy sculpting is rarely perfect on the first pass. As more forms are added, proportion checks and silhouette reviews become vital. A great artist remains flexible, adjusting underlying structures until the figure achieves both physical credibility and aesthetic appeal.

Rather than treating anatomy as a checklist of muscles and bones, successful modelers view it as an interconnected system, where each part influences the posture, tension, and balance of the whole.

Advanced Muscle Flow and Tissue Behavior

Understanding static anatomy is one milestone; mastering muscle flow and tissue behavior elevates sculpting to a professional standard. Muscles do not exist as rigid cables glued onto the skeleton. Instead, they stretch, compress, bulge, and twist in response to motion and tension.

Accurately depicting these behaviors requires a dynamic approach. Instead of sculpting muscles as independent shapes, artists must observe how groups of muscles interact based on motion or load. For instance, flexing the arm not only contracts the biceps but shifts neighboring muscles and even alters surface fat distribution.

When sculpting, professionals mimic this interconnectedness by softening transitions between muscles and by introducing natural deformation patterns. Sharp separations between muscle groups should only exist where underlying anatomical borders demand it, such as the clear break between the deltoid and pectoralis major.

Fatty tissues and skin layers also influence how muscles appear beneath the surface. Lean models, such as athletes, reveal sharp muscle definition, while models representing different body types require softer, rounder transitions. Ignoring these tissue behaviors leads to an unnatural and rigid appearance.

Advanced artists often create muscle flow studies before finalizing their sculpts. These studies involve isolating major motion lines across the body, mapping tension areas and relaxation zones. This planning step ensures that the final sculpt captures believable anatomy even in exaggerated or stylized designs.

Ultimately, understanding muscle flow is less about memorizing Latin names and more about studying how forces move through the body, shaping volume and structure in nuanced ways.

Hybridizing Real Anatomy for Creature Creation

Creature design is often misunderstood as an exercise in imagination alone. However, the most convincing creatures—whether dragons, aliens, or mythical beasts—are rooted in real anatomical logic. Hybridizing real anatomy offers a bridge between familiar biological rules and inventive fantasy designs.

The process starts by selecting base reference points. These could be multiple real-world species: combining the jaw structure of a crocodile, the hind legs of a kangaroo, and the wings of a bat, for instance. Each borrowed component must serve a plausible biological function in the creature's imagined environment.

One crucial principle is anatomical consistency. If a creature is designed with a heavy head, its neck and shoulder musculature must reflect the load-bearing adaptations seen in large real-world animals like buffalo or elephants. Similarly, flight-capable creatures need reinforced pectoral regions and correctly positioned wing structures relative to their center of gravity.

Joint placement and limb articulation must also follow rules of real-world movement. Designing a creature with backward-bending knees, for instance, demands understanding how digitigrade legs function in birds or cats. Otherwise, the design risks falling into visual confusion or mechanical implausibility.

Sculpting hybridized creatures often benefits from layering different animal references over a human anatomical framework first, especially if the goal is to maintain some degree of relatable proportions. This method provides an anchor for anatomical rules while allowing freedom to experiment with variations in form and function.

Hybrid anatomy is not about randomness; it is an informed blending of biological principles, ensuring that even the most imaginative designs feel grounded and believable.

Sculpting Dynamic Poses: Theory and Application

Dynamic posing transforms a model from a static figure into a story in motion. Achieving a convincing pose is not a matter of twisting limbs arbitrarily; it relies on weight distribution, balance, gesture, and tension—all guided by an understanding of how the body reacts to movement and gravity.

The first rule of dynamic posing is clarity of action. A viewer should be able to read a character's movement, intention, or emotion at a glance. This requires strong posing lines—flowing gestures that travel through the model's major masses (head, chest, pelvis, limbs) and direct the eye naturally.

Artists start with broad gestural sketches, sometimes called "action lines," that describe the energy of the pose before refining individual limbs or details. The spine acts as a primary line of motion, dictating how the upper and lower body relate during action.

Weight grounding is another critical element. One must visualize where the model's weight settles—on one leg, split across two, or projected forward in a leap. Improper weight distribution leads to floating, stiff, or broken-looking poses.

Compression and extension must be respected. In any real motion, parts of the body compress (shorten) while others extend (lengthen). A running figure, for example, will show compressed abdominal muscles on the side of the leading leg and stretched muscles on the opposite side.

Secondary motion adds authenticity. Hands, fingers, toes, tails, and clothing or equipment often lag behind the primary motion due to inertia, creating a sense of flow and time progression.

When applying dynamic poses in sculpting, it is often easier to start with a symmetrical, neutral base model and gradually break symmetry, moving from torso to limbs to extremities. Careful use of masking, Transpose tools, and deformation brushes enables fluid posing without damaging form integrity.

Dynamic posing is not just about adding drama—it is a discipline that breathes life into a sculpt, allowing characters and creatures to communicate without words.

High-Fidelity Polypainting and Texture Mastery

Painting Depth and Materials with Polypaint

True mastery of digital sculpting does not stop at form; it extends into the careful, deliberate layering of color and material illusion. Polypainting stands as one of the most direct and powerful methods to infuse a model with visual richness without relying on traditional UV textures.

Polypainting allows artists to apply color directly to the vertices of a high-resolution mesh. Each polygon holds color data, making the fidelity of the paintwork directly tied to mesh density. As such, before committing to final painting stages, it is essential to ensure the model contains enough subdivision levels to capture fine nuances.

A successful polypaint approach begins by blocking out the broadest color zones first. Large color transitions—such as the difference between flesh and armor, or skin and lips—must be mapped early. This creates a solid base foundation, ensuring later detailing sits within a believable context.

Once foundational colors are established, artists layer subtle variations, respecting material behavior. Skin, for example, is never a single flat tone; it contains shifts from reds to blues to yellows depending on blood flow, bone proximity, and exposure to light. Likewise, metals reflect highlights sharply while absorbing grime in recesses, and fabrics reveal subtle fiber patterns over their surfaces.

Layering transparent strokes with low-intensity brushes builds organic variation without muddying the underlying structure. It is not merely about adding detail, but about reinforcing the material quality being represented.

Clever use of masking based on cavity information allows artists to target painting to raised or recessed areas, helping simulate wear, grime accumulation, or surface fading naturally, without mechanical repetition.

Polypainting is a study in patience and observation, requiring artists to think in passes—building depth, material identity, and realism one careful stroke at a time.

UV Master Techniques for Flawless Textures

While polypainting offers speed and flexibility, complex production pipelines often require clean UV layouts for texture baking, export, and external rendering. Mastering UV workflows ensures that sculpted and painted details transfer seamlessly across platforms without distortion or artifacting.

The foundation of a flawless UV map lies in smart planning. Unwrapping should respect the flow of the model's structure, avoiding excessive stretching or compression. Natural seams should be hidden along less visible areas such as underarms, behind knees, or beneath clothing folds wherever possible.

Automated UV tools have grown increasingly sophisticated, but manual intervention remains critical for high-end work. Artists must oversee island placement, maintaining a balance between minimizing the number of seams and optimizing space usage within the UV square.

Once islands are laid out, proper packing maximizes resolution efficiency. Every pixel matters when baking maps at high resolutions, and wasted UV space translates into lost texture fidelity. Models should fill the UV grid intelligently, keeping related surfaces grouped logically to facilitate easier texture work later.

Correctly scaled and aligned UVs not only enhance texture quality but also make processes such as normal map baking and displacement map generation more predictable and cleaner. Inconsistent UV scaling leads to jagged details and visual breaks between different parts of the model.

Tools such as distortion visualization heatmaps can assist in diagnosing and correcting problem areas before moving into texturing stages, ensuring that all paintwork and material projections stay crisp and artifact-free.

UV mastery is not merely a technical hurdle; it is an artistic discipline that respects both the model's form and the final visual outcome.

Multi-Channel Texture Export and Application

Modern digital sculpting workflows demand more than just color maps. Surfaces are defined by a complex interplay of color, glossiness, roughness, metalness, normal details, displacement, and specular reflections. Exporting and managing multi-channel textures properly ensures that the final model carries its full richness into any rendering engine or game environment.

Preparation for multi-channel export begins within the sculpting software. Different types of data—such as polypaint (color), sculpted detail (normal or displacement), and material properties (specular, roughness, metallic)—must be isolated and captured individually.

When exporting color, polypaint can be baked directly into a texture map through UV mapping. Care must be taken to maintain sufficient resolution to preserve fine details, especially for high-resolution sculpts. Normal maps extract high-frequency sculpt details into low-poly versions without losing surface richness. Meanwhile, displacement maps carry actual height information, critical for close-up renders where silhouette integrity matters.

For physical-based rendering pipelines, additional channels such as roughness and metallic maps must be prepared, often using a combination of manual painting and procedural generation. Each map must be tested independently to ensure clean transitions, avoiding pixel-level noise that could compromise realism.

File naming conventions, color space management (linear vs. sRGB), and proper bit-depth settings (such as 16-bit for displacements) must all be handled carefully to maintain fidelity across different platforms.

Finally, texture maps must be reassembled within the target engine or renderer. Whether applied in Blender, Unreal Engine, or other environments, correct channel plugging and shader configuration determine whether the textures faithfully reproduce the artist's intended look.

Multi-channel texture export is not an afterthought—it is an integral stage that ensures sculptural and painting efforts translate into polished, production-ready assets.

Painting Stylized vs Photorealistic Models

Not all projects demand photorealism. Stylized models, often seen in animation, mobile games, or illustrative work, require a completely different painting philosophy than models aimed at hyper-real accuracy.

Photorealistic painting mimics the chaotic imperfection of real surfaces. Fine color variations, tiny imperfections, noise, grime accumulation, and subtle lighting interplay create a world that feels tactile and tangible. It relies on capturing randomness without losing control—adding barely perceptible asymmetries and texture breaks that fool the eye into accepting the model as "real."

Stylized painting, on the other hand, embraces clarity, exaggeration, and abstraction. Colors are often cleaner, with deliberate simplifications of shading and material transitions. Light and shadow boundaries may be emphasized to read strongly from a distance. Surface textures may suggest material type without overwhelming the core silhouette or color scheme.

When painting stylized models, artists often think in terms of shape and contrast rather than pure realism. Techniques such as hand-painting shadow accents, color gradients, and outline stylizations support the overall design readability.

Importantly, even within stylization, material logic should not be abandoned. Metals should still feel metallic, skin should still feel organic, even if both are represented with far simpler shapes and color palettes.

Artists moving between styles must adjust their brushwork, color theory, and even stroke rhythm. While photorealistic texturing rewards patience and layering, stylized painting often demands confident, deliberate mark-making and stronger color choices.

Mastery lies in understanding the expectations of the target visual style and adapting techniques to achieve it without confusion or hesitation.

Advanced Subtool Management and Optimization

Intelligent Subtool Hierarchies

Handling complex digital models requires more than artistic skill; it demands a sharp organizational strategy. As projects grow in complexity, managing individual elements becomes critical for efficiency, clarity, and performance.

Intelligent subtool hierarchy begins with deliberate planning. Each significant component of a model—such as armor plates, clothing, weapons, anatomical parts, or accessories—should occupy its own subtool. Grouping these elements separately avoids confusion and allows focused editing without the risk of unintended alterations to other parts of the model.

Naming conventions play a vital role. Clear, descriptive names for each subtool prevent the disorganization that often plagues heavy projects. A consistent structure—such as using prefixes like "Body_Arm_L" or "Armor_Shoulder_R"—allows for rapid navigation, batch operations, and error prevention.

Beyond individual subtools, logical grouping must consider functional relationships. Hierarchies should reflect the physical or conceptual structure of the model. For example, all components of a character's outfit might be grouped separately from their body, while weapons and props are categorized independently. This modular thinking prepares the project for easier posing, material assignment, and later export for rigging or rendering.

Subtools that form symmetrical parts should be kept separate where possible. This allows artists to work on one side, duplicate, and mirror changes without unnecessary complications.

An effective hierarchy not only simplifies the artistic process but also lays the groundwork for collaboration. Well-organized projects enable multiple artists to understand, modify, and optimize assets with minimal ramp-up time.

Good hierarchy management is a discipline in itself, requiring constant upkeep, but the reward is a faster, cleaner, and more controlled production workflow.

Performance Optimization for Heavy Scenes

As models become more detailed and scenes grow heavier, performance challenges can bottleneck even the most powerful systems. Understanding how to manage resources efficiently is key to keeping the creative process fluid and responsive.

One primary optimization strategy is the intelligent use of subdivision levels. High-resolution details should be reserved for final stages of sculpting. Early shaping work should happen on lower subdivision levels, switching to higher levels only when necessary. This approach significantly reduces memory overhead and improves viewport responsiveness.

Hiding unnecessary subtools during heavy operations minimizes processing load. When not actively working on a part, it is best to hide or temporarily delete higher subdivision levels using non-destructive methods, ensuring that only necessary geometry remains in memory.

Decimating non-deforming or secondary objects provides another optimization route. Items like weapons, armor pieces, or mechanical elements often do not require multi-million polygon counts. Controlled decimation reduces polycount while preserving surface detail, allowing for lighter scenes without visible loss in quality.

Splitting high-density models into separate subtools can also alleviate processing stress. Instead of managing a single, massive object, the system handles multiple smaller ones more efficiently.

Another critical practice is managing undo history. As sculpting sessions grow longer, undo stacks become massive memory drains. Saving incremental versions of the file and purging old undo history periodically keeps sessions nimble.

Background processes, unnecessary real-time effects, and heavy preview shaders should be minimized during active sculpting sessions. A lighter shader or basic material reduces strain on the graphics processor, allowing for smoother navigation and manipulation.

Ultimately, consistent, mindful optimization practices ensure that the tool remains an extension of the artist's intent rather than a barrier to creativity.

Effective Use of Folders and Subtool Master Tips

Folders within the subtool stack offer a powerful but often underutilized method for maintaining order and streamlining complex workflows. Proper folder usage creates intuitive, collapsible groupings that mirror logical project divisions.

Creating folders for major model sections—such as "Headgear," "Torso," "Accessories," and "Weapons"—enables artists to isolate entire categories with a single click. This not only helps visual organization but also allows for mass visibility toggles, quick duplication, group exports, and batch processing.

Folders can serve as mini-projects within a larger piece. By grouping associated subtools together, tasks such as local posing, material application, and focused detailing become more manageable. Instead of scrolling through dozens or hundreds of subtools, an artist can work within a focused subset at any time.

In addition to folders, specialized plugins and toolsets designed for subtool management offer tremendous advantages. Features such as batch renaming, group duplication, smart merging, and layer flattening save countless hours during production.

Subtool Master, a well-known utility, empowers users to perform operations across multiple subtools simultaneously. Actions such as mirror, merge, rename, export, and subdivide become streamlined, reducing repetitive manual tasks and potential errors. When combined with smart folder structures, these tools can supercharge productivity across even the most demanding projects.

Using such tools effectively requires a disciplined workflow. Artists must maintain consistent naming, hierarchy, and grouping from the beginning rather than waiting until the project becomes unwieldy.

Efficient subtool management, intelligent folder use, and mastery of batch operations do not just tidy up projects—they empower artists to focus on creation rather than technical navigation. A well-structured project breathes clarity and confidence into every stage of production.

Displacement, Normal, and Vector Maps: Expert Tactics

High-End Map Extraction

The creation of high-quality displacement, normal, and vector maps is an integral part of modern digital sculpting workflows. These maps allow artists to translate intricate surface detail from high-resolution models into low-resolution geometry, preserving the appearance of fine details without incurring the performance overhead associated with dense meshes.

Displacement maps, in particular, allow for precise surface detail on low-polygon meshes by using grayscale images to drive geometry changes during rendering. To extract high-quality displacement maps, it's essential to consider the resolution, precision, and method used during the baking process.

One of the most effective ways to extract a displacement map is through the use of a high-resolution model, ensuring that the sculpted details—such as wrinkles, pores, and fine textures—are captured. To begin, it's important to adjust the **subdivision levels** of the model, as the highest level should be used to retain all of the fine details. Tools for map extraction, whether inside a sculpting application or through external programs, must be configured for **accurate resolution scaling** and **appropriate edge padding** to avoid seams and artifacts.

A common mistake in map extraction occurs when **detail is lost** due to insufficient resolution or incorrect settings during the baking process. A map should be baked in a resolution high enough to retain all necessary detail, but not too high that it becomes impractical for the target environment. For instance, a 4K displacement map may offer impressive details for a close-up render, but for real-time applications like video games, a lower-resolution map is often preferred to maintain performance.

It's also important to ensure that the **target mesh's UVs** are properly laid out, with no overlapping or stretched areas. This will ensure the detail from the high-poly mesh translates seamlessly onto the low-poly geometry.

Additionally, **normal maps** are essential for simulating surface detail on low-resolution models by using RGB values to represent surface directions, allowing for the appearance of depth without the need for actual geometry. Normal map extraction is similar to displacement maps but focuses on surface orientation rather than actual geometry. Both types of maps should be extracted at the highest possible resolution for the finest detail, and it is beneficial to use multiple passes to capture different levels of detail (e.g., a base pass and a fine detail pass).

For **vector maps**, which are used to capture directional information for complex details, similar principles apply. However, these maps go beyond surface detailing and represent more advanced, vector-based displacement, allowing for even more complex variations in surface treatment.

Correcting and Refining Displacement Data

After extraction, **displacement maps** often require fine-tuning to ensure they provide the intended results across different environments. Displacement data can sometimes exhibit undesirable artifacts, such as **hard edges**, **seams**, or **blurring** where the map is applied to lower-resolution geometry. To correct these issues, it is essential to understand the relationship between the extracted map and the model's surface.

One common technique for refining displacement maps is **adjusting the depth range**. This can be done by tweaking the **contrast and levels** in the map to ensure that the displacement is correctly applied during rendering. Sometimes, subtle adjustments to the map's grayscale values can help remove the unwanted artifacts while preserving the fine details that make the model realistic.

When working with large, complex maps, **tiling issues** may also arise. These are often visible at the seams or edges where the texture is applied repetitively. To address this, **seamless tiling** techniques should be implemented to ensure smooth transitions between tiles, preventing any noticeable borders or breaks in the displacement.

Additionally, **subdivision adjustments** can be made to the low-poly mesh during the rendering process to accommodate more complex displacements without distortion. In these cases, **adaptive subdivision** techniques can dynamically adjust the resolution of the mesh during rendering, preserving the integrity of the displacement data without overburdening the system with unnecessary polygons.

Another useful technique is **extrapolation**, which can extend the displacement data beyond the edges of the map to cover areas where the original extraction may have been incomplete or inaccurate. Refining vector maps for more advanced detail may require adjusting the vector directions to match the geometry more accurately, ensuring that complex surface textures like skin pores, wrinkles, or fabric folds are portrayed correctly.

Multi-Map Exporter Workflows for Major Pipelines (Maya, Unreal Engine, Blender)

In professional pipelines, it's not uncommon to export multiple maps for a single model. The key challenge lies in ensuring that these maps are compatible with the tools and rendering engines used at various stages of production. Whether working in **Maya**, **Unreal Engine**, **Blender**, or other software, understanding how to properly export multiple maps for seamless integration is essential.

Maya:

When exporting displacement and normal maps from **Maya**, the process typically involves using **Arnold**, **V-Ray**, or other third-party rendering engines. In Maya, **Arnold's AI Standard Surface shader** supports high-quality displacement mapping, and displacement maps can be assigned using the **displacement shader node**.

To ensure accuracy, artists must be sure to match the **resolution of the map** to the render size and adjust the **subdivision settings** of the mesh to match the level of detail required. Maya's **File Texture** node allows for easy exporting of multiple texture maps, including displacement, normal, and vector maps, in a manner that can be easily integrated into the rendering pipeline.

Unreal Engine:

For real-time applications like **Unreal Engine**, normal and displacement maps are crucial for achieving high-quality visuals while maintaining performance. Unreal Engine primarily uses **normal maps** to create the illusion of high-resolution surface detail without the heavy cost of complex geometry. In contrast to displacement maps, which are used in ray-traced or offline renders, normal maps are processed at runtime, making them ideal for game engines.

When exporting from **ZBrush** or another sculpting application, normal maps should be baked at the **highest resolution possible**, while displacement maps should be optimized for real-time performance (usually at lower resolutions). Unreal Engine also supports **tessellation** for displacement, which can further enhance the appearance of detail at runtime by subdividing the model's surface based on the displacement map.

Blender:

Blender, known for its versatility, supports both normal and displacement maps in its default rendering system, **Cycles**, as well as in the **Eevee** real-time renderer. When exporting multiple maps from Blender, artists should ensure the appropriate **UV unwrapping** is in place to prevent any texture stretching or seams.

Blender's native tools allow for **multi-channel exporting**, which enables the artist to export all necessary maps (displacement, normal, and vector) in one workflow. The **Multi-res Modifier** is often used to handle displacement maps, enabling high-resolution sculpting and rendering without hitting memory limits.

To optimize Blender for high-fidelity textures and maps, it's crucial to **bake** displacement and normal maps at higher subdivisions and then apply them to the low-poly model for rendering. Blender supports **texture painting** to refine these maps, ensuring that the details remain intact during export.

Custom Brushes, Macros, and Plugins

Creating Industry-Grade Custom Brushes

In the world of digital sculpting, custom brushes serve as invaluable tools that enable artists to efficiently create unique textures, intricate details, and complex surfaces. The ability to craft custom brushes tailored to specific needs is an essential skill for any advanced user. Custom brushes provide a level of control and flexibility that can elevate your workflow, allowing for faster and more precise sculpting.

To create industry-grade custom brushes, the first step is understanding the underlying mechanics of how brushes interact with the model. Custom brushes are made by combining **alphas** (grayscale images used to define the brush shape) with specific settings that control how they interact with the surface. In sculpting programs like ZBrush, artists can modify key brush parameters, such as **size, intensity, flow, and focal shift**, to adapt the brush to different surfaces and sculpting techniques.

One of the most important aspects of creating a custom brush is defining its **alpha shape**. This can be done by using an image editor to create a high-quality grayscale image that represents the texture or detail you want to imprint on the model. These alphas can be anything from the rough texture of a rock to the fine pores of skin or the sharp ridges of a mechanical surface. Once the alpha is ready, it can be loaded into the brush system, where you can further adjust settings like the **depth, noise, and directionality** to enhance its functionality.

A key feature of custom brushes is the ability to combine multiple alphas into a single brush. For instance, a **combination of different surface textures** can be blended together to create a more complex and dynamic brush, allowing you to quickly sculpt a variety of details in one pass. Additionally, **surface noise** can be incorporated into brushes to create organic variations, adding realism to sculpted forms.

To maintain efficiency, **brush presets** can be saved for reuse, meaning you can tailor brushes to specific projects or environments. It's also crucial to continuously **test** your custom brushes on the model to make sure they interact with the surface correctly, producing the desired effect without introducing unwanted artifacts or distortions.

Lastly, **custom brushes** can be enhanced by using them in conjunction with other advanced sculpting tools, such as **Alpha Blending**, which allows you to mix different alphas and create new, hybrid brush effects.

Building Time-Saving Macros for Sculpting Pipelines

Macros are a powerful way to automate repetitive tasks within your sculpting workflow. These time-saving scripts allow artists to **record sequences of actions** and replay them instantly with a single click. This is particularly beneficial when working on complex models or in large production environments where efficiency is critical.

The process of building macros starts with understanding the basic functionality of the sculpting software's macro system. Most digital sculpting programs, such as ZBrush, offer a built-in macro recorder that allows you to **record a series of steps**, such as brush strokes, camera movements, or tool selections. Once recorded, these actions can be assigned to a hotkey or button, streamlining your process by eliminating the need to manually repeat those actions every time.

To ensure your macros are effective, they should be designed with **modularity** in mind. This means creating macros that focus on specific tasks rather than trying to record a broad range of actions in a single macro. For instance, a macro for creating base meshes can be separated from a macro that applies detailing to the surface. This approach allows for greater flexibility and makes it easier to troubleshoot if something goes wrong.

One of the key benefits of using macros is the ability to **standardize workflows** across multiple team members. In professional environments, creating macros for common actions like setting up brushes, aligning the camera, or switching between tools can save considerable time, especially when multiple artists are involved in a project. By sharing macros among team members, you ensure that everyone is following the same processes, reducing variability and improving consistency across assets.

Moreover, macros can be further enhanced by incorporating **conditional logic**, which allows for more dynamic workflows. This enables you to build macros that react differently based on certain conditions, such as the specific type of object being sculpted or the current brush settings.

Must-Have Plugins and How to Customize Them

Plugins are another essential component of an efficient digital sculpting pipeline. These external tools extend the functionality of your sculpting software, offering additional features, shortcuts, and automation that can significantly enhance your creative process. There is an abundance of plugins available for digital sculpting programs, each designed to streamline specific tasks, from topology cleanup to rendering optimizations.

When selecting plugins, it's important to identify which tools **align with your workflow** and **address your specific needs**. For example, **Dynamesh** is a popular plugin in ZBrush that allows you to easily create a uniform mesh density for your sculpt, facilitating smoother detailing. Similarly, plugins like **Subtool Master** help manage large numbers of subtools efficiently, enabling you to group, duplicate, and merge them with ease.

Another must-have plugin for many advanced users is a **UV Master**, which simplifies the process of unwrapping complex 3D models into flat UVs. By automating much of the UV mapping process, this plugin saves time and reduces the likelihood of errors, which can be difficult to fix later in the production pipeline.

For those working in animation or game design, plugins that offer **retopology tools** are invaluable. These plugins allow for automatic or semi-automatic generation of low-poly meshes based on high-resolution sculpts, ensuring that models maintain their visual fidelity while being optimized for performance.

In addition to pre-built plugins, one of the most powerful aspects of plugins is the ability to **customize them** to fit your specific workflow. Many digital sculpting programs allow you to create or modify plugins through scripting or configuration files. By learning how to write custom scripts or tweak existing ones, you can adapt a plugin to address unique project requirements. This customization can range from changing the user interface layout to creating entirely new tools that automate complex sequences of actions.

Customizing Plugins:

To customize plugins effectively, you should be familiar with the scripting languages used by your sculpting software. For instance, **ZBrush** uses **ZScript**, a scripting language that allows users to extend the functionality of the program by writing custom scripts. These scripts can create new tools, modify existing ones, or integrate with third-party software.

Maya, another popular tool for 3D modeling and sculpting, uses **MEL** (Maya Embedded Language) or **Python** for scripting. This flexibility allows users to create custom tools, automate repetitive tasks, and streamline their workflow. If you're working in a team, it's often beneficial to create plugins that conform to the team's specific production pipeline, ensuring that everything runs smoothly across different departments.

For those working in **Blender**, the open-source nature of the software allows for extensive plugin customization through **Python scripting**. Blender's flexible API allows you to build complex tools, automate rigging processes, or even create new rendering techniques, all of which can be customized to meet project-specific requirements.

The key to customizing plugins successfully is understanding the underlying workflow that the plugin aims to address. By analyzing the steps involved in a particular task and identifying areas where automation can save time or improve efficiency, you can tailor plugins to meet the specific needs of your pipeline.

ZBrush to External Pipelines: A Professional Workflow

Preparing Models for Unreal, Unity, Blender, and Maya

In a professional pipeline, the ability to seamlessly transfer your sculpted models from ZBrush to external applications such as Unreal Engine, Unity, Blender, and Maya is crucial. These programs each have their own requirements and best practices, but there are common steps that can help ensure your assets transfer smoothly, maintaining their high-quality details while optimizing them for game engines or animation software.

Unreal Engine: Preparing Models for Optimal Performance

When preparing models for Unreal Engine, the focus is typically on both visual fidelity and performance. Unreal Engine uses a combination of high-poly models, normal maps, and optimized geometry for rendering. Here's how to prepare a ZBrush model for Unreal:

1. **Retopology**: Before exporting, make sure your model is retopologized to create a low-poly version of the mesh. Unreal Engine handles low-poly models much more efficiently than high-poly models, so it's essential to optimize geometry. Use ZBrush's **ZRemesher** or **Dynamesh** for creating a cleaner base mesh, and retopologize for better animation support.

2. **Normal and Displacement Maps**: Unreal supports both normal and displacement maps for adding detail to low-poly models. After retopologizing your model, use ZBrush's **SubTool** features to generate normal maps and displacement maps that will maintain the fine details of the original high-poly mesh.

3. **UV Unwrapping**: Ensure your model is correctly unwrapped for texturing. Unreal Engine requires UVs to be clean and non-overlapping, with a reasonable texel density. ZBrush's **UV Master** plugin can

streamline this process, helping you achieve precise UV layouts before exporting.

4. **Exporting the Model**: Export the model from ZBrush in a format Unreal supports, such as **FBX**. When exporting, check the **export settings** to ensure that both the high-poly and low-poly meshes are included, and that normal and displacement maps are correctly assigned.

Unity: Optimizing for Real-Time Rendering

Unity, like Unreal Engine, is widely used for creating real-time 3D content, particularly in game development. The process for preparing models in Unity is similar but has its nuances:

1. **Low-Poly and High-Poly Models**: Unity requires the same balance between high-poly detail and low-poly efficiency. To prepare for Unity, first ensure that your model has been properly retopologized in ZBrush. The low-poly version should be used in Unity for real-time rendering, while the high-poly version is used for baking maps.

2. **Baking High-Resolution Details**: Use ZBrush to create high-resolution details and bake them into normal maps and ambient occlusion maps. Unity uses these baked textures to simulate high-level detail on a low-poly mesh, saving on performance while maintaining visual quality.

3. **Texturing and Shading**: Unity supports the **PBR (Physically Based Rendering)** workflow, which is essential for creating realistic materials and textures. When exporting textures from ZBrush, ensure they are in a PBR-friendly format such as **Roughness, Metallic, and Normal maps**. You can use **Polygroups** in ZBrush to help with UV mapping, ensuring the UVs are laid out in a way that works well with Unity's texture painting tools.

4. **Optimizing for Performance**: Unity's performance relies on several factors including polycount, texture sizes, and shaders. When exporting

your assets from ZBrush, make sure to follow Unity's polycount limits for real-time performance. Also, consider **Level of Detail (LOD)** optimization to provide multiple versions of the model for different distances in the game environment.

Blender: From ZBrush to the Open-Source Environment

Blender is an open-source 3D creation suite that supports a wide range of features for sculpting, modeling, texturing, and rendering. When transferring your ZBrush model to Blender, the workflow is centered around preserving details while maintaining ease of manipulation for animation, rigging, and rendering:

1. **Exporting for Blender**: ZBrush's **FBX** export works well for Blender, but for more control over the transfer, you may prefer **OBJ** or **Alembic** formats, especially when dealing with multiple subtools or high-resolution meshes.

2. **Sculpting to Retopology**: Once the model is in Blender, you can further refine the topology if needed, especially if the original mesh wasn't fully retopologized in ZBrush. Blender's **Remesh** and **Retopology** tools provide an easy way to add quads and optimize your geometry for animation.

3. **UV Mapping and Textures**: If your ZBrush UVs are not perfect, Blender provides robust tools for **UV unwrapping**. Blender's **node-based shader editor** allows you to work with textures generated in ZBrush, including displacement maps, normals, and color maps.

4. **Polishing the Model**: Use Blender's sculpting tools to further refine the model or correct any issues after exporting. Additionally, Blender's **Grease Pencil** and **Sculpt Mode** provide powerful methods to add further detail and refinement.

Maya: Precision and Control for Animation and VFX

Maya, a leader in animation and VFX, is frequently used to create models that will be rigged, animated, or integrated into complex scenes. Preparing models in Maya involves ensuring proper topology, UV mapping, and efficient exportation of textures and geometry:

1. **Retopology for Rigging**: Maya relies heavily on clean, quads-based geometry for rigging and animation. Exporting models directly from ZBrush without retopologizing can lead to problematic rigs or distortions during animation. Use ZBrush to create a retopologized mesh or export high-resolution meshes for use in Maya's **Tesselate** tool for further refinement.

2. **UV Layout**: Maya's **UV editor** allows for intricate adjustments to your UVs, so if needed, you can adjust any imperfections in the UV layout. ZBrush's **UV Master** can help streamline this process, but it's still important to make sure that Maya's UV tools are properly utilized.

3. **Exporting for Maya**: When exporting for Maya, **FBX** is usually the preferred format. Ensure you export only the relevant meshes and ensure that the export settings for textures and vertex colors are correctly configured.

Exporting High Fidelity Without Compromise

When transferring models from ZBrush to external applications, maintaining high fidelity is essential to ensure the sculpt retains its detail, quality, and appearance. The key steps to achieving this are:

1. **High-Poly to Low-Poly Baking**: Baking high-resolution details from ZBrush onto a low-poly mesh ensures that the intricate sculptural features are maintained in the final asset. Export high-poly models from ZBrush

and bake them into normal, displacement, and ambient occlusion maps for use in other programs.

2. **Use of Displacement and Normal Maps**: Displacement maps are used to modify the geometry of the mesh, while normal maps simulate surface detail without altering the mesh. Both are critical for retaining the high-level detail of the sculpt when the model is used in game engines or rendered for animation.

3. **Texture Resolution**: Ensure that textures are of a sufficient resolution to maintain clarity in the final render or real-time application. ZBrush supports high-resolution textures, and exporting them at the correct resolution ensures that they appear sharp and detailed in other programs.

4. **File Compression and Optimization**: When exporting models to external programs, it's essential to keep file sizes manageable. This includes optimizing texture maps and meshes for efficient rendering in external applications. Ensure that textures are in formats that support high-quality details without bloating file sizes, such as **TIF** or **PNG** for color maps, and **EXR** for displacement.

Cross-Application Polishing (Substance, Marmoset, Blender)

Once your model is exported into another application, cross-application polishing can refine it further, ensuring it meets the final production standards for visual quality.

1. **Substance Painter**: Substance Painter excels at adding detailed textures using a **PBR workflow**. Import your models from ZBrush into Substance to add wear, dirt, rust, and other surface details. Use advanced materials and smart materials to create complex, realistic textures that seamlessly fit into the game or animation pipeline.

2. **Marmoset Toolbag**: After creating your textures, Marmoset Toolbag is an excellent tool for rendering the final model. It allows you to quickly preview the model with high-quality real-time rendering, adjusting materials, lighting, and cameras to polish your asset for final presentation.

3. **Blender**: Blender's **Cycles** rendering engine offers an excellent environment to fine-tune lighting, shadows, and textures after your model has been imported. Blender can also be used to adjust any final details or add further refinements in sculpting or shading before final rendering.

Rendering Masterclass: Turning Sculptures into Art

In digital sculpture, the transition from raw geometry to a finished piece of art is often marked by the rendering process. Rendering is where the technicality of 3D modeling merges with the artistry of visualization. Whether you are working with advanced tools like KeyShot or using ZBrush's BPR (Best Preview Render), achieving a realistic or stylistically compelling final image is not just about creating the model itself but also about setting the scene, lighting, and enhancing the final output in post-production. This chapter focuses on advanced rendering workflows, lighting theory, and compositing techniques to help you turn your digital sculptures into stunning works of art.

Advanced KeyShot and ZBrush BPR Workflows

KeyShot Workflow for High-Quality Renders

KeyShot is one of the most widely used rendering engines in the 3D industry for creating photorealistic images. Its simplicity and speed make it ideal for rendering intricate digital sculptures. Understanding how to set up an effective workflow can save you significant time while maximizing output quality.

1. **Importing Models**: The first step in the KeyShot workflow is to import your 3D model. KeyShot supports various formats such as **OBJ**, **FBX**, and **STL**. The model should be properly UV-unwrapped in ZBrush or any other modeling software before importing. Ensure that the scale is correct to avoid any unexpected results when lighting and texturing the model.

2. **Material Setup**: KeyShot offers a vast library of materials, but to make your sculpture truly stand out, you need to tailor the materials to the unique qualities of your model. Adjust the **reflection**, **refraction**, **roughness**, and **bump mapping** for each material to ensure that the

sculptural details are accurately conveyed. Adding textures to your materials, such as **wood**, **metal**, or **stone**, can provide a more lifelike or stylized look, depending on the style you're aiming for.

3. **Lighting Setup**: Lighting is one of the most crucial aspects of rendering. KeyShot allows you to add custom lighting using HDRI images or point and area lights. An essential technique is to place **light sources** strategically to enhance the details of your sculpture. For example, a **three-point lighting setup** is often used to highlight the form while avoiding overexposure in any part of the model.

4. **Render Settings**: KeyShot uses real-time rendering, meaning you can see your changes instantly. However, for final renders, it's important to adjust the **render quality settings**. Choose higher quality settings for the final output, but keep in mind that this will increase rendering time. You can also enable **depth of field** to add focus and blur effects to the background, enhancing the realism of the render.

5. **Post-Processing**: Once the render is complete, you can enhance the final output using KeyShot's **Post Effects**. Effects like **bloom**, **glare**, and **vignetting** can add an artistic touch and make the image feel more polished and refined. Adjusting the exposure and color balance can also help fine-tune the final look.

ZBrush BPR Workflow for Realistic Previews

ZBrush's Best Preview Render (BPR) is a powerful tool for quickly generating high-quality renders directly from the software. While it may not match the photorealism of external render engines like KeyShot, it can still produce excellent results when used effectively.

1. **Preparing the Model**: Before rendering in ZBrush, ensure your model is fully prepared. This includes checking the sculpt for any visible errors or seams, ensuring UVs are laid out properly, and having displacement and normal maps baked where necessary. ZBrush allows you to export these

maps later for use in external applications.

2. **Lighting and Shadows**: The BPR system in ZBrush gives you control over light sources, shadows, and ambient occlusion. You can add multiple lights, each with its own intensity, color, and angle. Using **soft shadows** can help create more natural results, while hard shadows can add dramatic contrast. BPR's **Shadow settings** also offer customizable **shadow opacity** and **softness** to further refine the lighting effects.

3. **Materials and Polygroups**: ZBrush allows you to assign different materials to different parts of your model using **Polygroups**. For rendering, each material can be customized for greater realism, adjusting properties like **specularity**, **glossiness**, and **ambient occlusion**. The choice of material is important when looking to emphasize certain details of your model. For example, applying a **matte** material to skin or a **metallic** material to armor will yield distinct visual results.

4. **Rendering and Adjustments**: After setting up your model, lighting, and materials, use the **BPR Render** button to start the render process. ZBrush allows you to preview the lighting and shading in real-time, adjusting as needed to achieve the right look. You can also use **render passes**, such as **ZDepth**, **Normal**, and **AO** passes, to separate elements for better control in post-production.

Lighting Theory for Digital Sculptures

Lighting is arguably the most important element when transforming a 3D model into a finished piece of art. Good lighting will not only highlight your sculpture's most important details but also create mood, atmosphere, and realism.

The Fundamentals of Lighting

To fully understand how to light your sculpture effectively, it's important to know the basic principles of lighting:

1. **Key Light**: The primary light source, this should be the brightest and most directional light. The key light defines the form of the sculpture and casts the strongest shadows. The angle of the key light can drastically change the way the model is perceived.

2. **Fill Light**: A secondary light used to soften shadows created by the key light. The fill light should be much softer and less intense, often positioned opposite the key light.

3. **Rim or Back Light**: This light is positioned behind the sculpture to create highlights along the edges. It helps to separate the model from the background and adds depth, making it appear more three-dimensional.

Lighting Styles

Different lighting setups can significantly affect the mood of the scene. Below are common setups used in digital sculpture rendering:

1. **Three-Point Lighting**: This is the classic approach, using a combination of key, fill, and backlights. It is particularly effective for portrait-style sculptures and helps create a balanced look.

2. **Dramatic Lighting**: By using strong contrasts and harsh shadows, dramatic lighting can add a sense of mystery or power to a sculpture. This setup typically uses only a key light and a backlight, leaving deep shadows in the fill regions.

3. **Ambient Lighting**: This type of lighting does not create distinct shadows but instead evenly lights the sculpture. It's useful for showcasing smooth, featureless surfaces or when you want a more neutral or calm atmosphere.

4. **Natural Lighting**: Mimicking the lighting found in nature (such as sunlight or moonlight), this setup tends to have a more diffuse quality and soft shadows, making it ideal for organic models like plants, animals, or human figures.

Compositing Render Passes in Photoshop and Beyond

Once the rendering process is complete, compositing allows you to further refine the image, enhancing details, adjusting colors, and adding special effects that elevate the final result.

Render Passes

Render passes are separate elements of the scene that can be rendered independently and later combined to create a complete image. Here are the most common passes used for compositing:

1. **Beauty Pass**: This is the primary pass, containing the final look of the model with all materials, lighting, and textures applied.

2. **ZDepth Pass**: This pass stores information about the distance of each object from the camera. It's useful for adding depth effects like **depth of field** and **atmospheric perspective** in post-production.

3. **Normal Pass**: The normal pass contains surface normals, which can be used to add or adjust the lighting and shading in specific areas of the model, giving you more control over how the model interacts with light in the final composition.

4. **Ambient Occlusion (AO) Pass**: AO helps simulate shadows in creases and areas where objects are close together. It can be used to add realism to the model and accentuate details that might be overlooked in the beauty

pass.

5. **Specular Pass**: This pass isolates the specular reflections from the rest of the lighting and can be used to tweak the intensity and spread of highlights on your model.

6. **Shadow Pass**: This contains just the shadows from the scene and can be used to fine-tune shadow intensity or add additional shadow effects without altering the rest of the image.

Compositing in Photoshop

Once you have all the necessary passes, you can bring them into Photoshop or another image editing program to begin compositing.

1. **Layering Passes**: Start by combining your beauty pass with the other passes. Adjust the opacity of each pass to control how much influence each one has on the final image. For instance, you can blend the AO pass with the beauty pass to enhance shadows in tight areas.

2. **Color Grading**: Use Photoshop's adjustment layers to modify the overall color scheme. **Curves**, **Hue/Saturation**, and **Selective Color** are excellent tools to correct colors or apply a specific mood to the scene.

3. **Add Effects**: Finally, you can enhance the image with visual effects. This may include adding **lens flares, glows**, or **bokeh effects** to simulate real-world camera behavior. Textures, gradients, and other artistic flourishes can also help create the desired atmosphere for the sculpture.

Cutting-Edge Features and Experimental Techniques

The digital sculpting landscape is continually evolving, with new tools, technologies, and innovations being introduced every year. For artists and professionals, staying ahead of the curve means adopting and experimenting with the latest features and techniques that push the boundaries of what's possible. This chapter explores some of the most exciting and experimental developments in digital sculpting, specifically focusing on ZBrush innovations, AI integration, and procedural sculpting. These tools not only improve the efficiency and creativity of your workflow but also open up new creative possibilities.

Utilizing the Latest ZBrush Innovations (Updated for 2025)

As digital sculpting continues to evolve, ZBrush, a leader in the industry, has introduced several powerful features that enhance both the technical and artistic aspects of the sculpting process. Staying up-to-date with the newest updates ensures that your workflow remains efficient, effective, and competitive.

Dynamic Subdivision and Mesh Density Control

One of the most significant updates to ZBrush in 2025 is the refinement of its **dynamic subdivision** system. This feature allows artists to work with models at multiple levels of detail without the need to worry about the computational overhead of traditional subdivisions. ZBrush now offers more control over mesh density, allowing you to increase the detail of only certain regions of the model while keeping the rest of the model at a lower resolution. This approach ensures that you can maintain high performance even when working with complex assets, making it ideal for both large-scale and detailed projects.

Dynamic subdivision significantly enhances the sculpting process by allowing you to focus on specific areas of your model, adding high-frequency details where needed while preserving computational resources for other areas. This results in smoother, more responsive sculpting and the ability to work with larger, more complex models without compromising performance.

Procedural Brushes and Customizable UI

ZBrush's **procedural brushes** have been improved with a range of new settings that allow for more flexibility in creating and applying custom brushes. These brushes can now be influenced by procedural patterns, randomization, and even external inputs like sounds or images. This means that an artist can create complex textures, fine details, or surface irregularities without manually sculpting every aspect. Procedural brushes can make your workflow faster and more organic, allowing for a more free-flowing and dynamic sculpting experience.

Additionally, ZBrush's **user interface (UI)** has undergone further customization, allowing users to modify the workspace to suit their specific needs. New features, such as **snap-to-grid** and **workspace mirroring**, allow for greater efficiency and accuracy when setting up the sculpting environment. Artists can now tailor the software to fit their individual preferences, making the sculpting process more intuitive and personalized.

Polygrouping and Masking Enhancements

The updates to **polygroups** and **masking** in 2025 make it easier to isolate specific areas of your model for detailed work. With advanced tools for masking and grouping polygons based on their topological features, you can now create more complex shapes and manipulate individual areas with more control. This includes the ability to mask parts of a model automatically based on the curvature or the edge flow, simplifying tasks like detailing small crevices or intricate designs.

ZBrush's **automatic polygroups** can intelligently create groups based on your model's geometry, making it easier to apply specific effects to parts of the model. This system eliminates much of the manual work previously required for separating elements, speeding up the workflow considerably.

Real-Time Rendering Enhancements

ZBrush has also improved its **real-time rendering** capabilities. While its main focus remains on sculpting, ZBrush's ability to preview models in a rendered state has been taken to new heights. New render settings, such as **light simulation** and **global illumination**, help create realistic lighting effects within the ZBrush environment, allowing you to make informed decisions while sculpting. Artists can preview the final look of their models as they work, making the process smoother and less time-consuming.

Experimenting with Sculpting AI Integration

Artificial intelligence (AI) has become increasingly integrated into the creative process, offering tools that speed up workflows, enhance realism, and provide new possibilities for artists. In digital sculpting, AI is being used in several innovative ways to assist with procedural generation, surface detail, and even stylistic changes.

AI-Assisted Surface Detailing

AI tools in sculpting software can now automatically add surface detail based on an artist's intent. By analyzing the model, AI can add textures like **skin pores**, **fabric wrinkles**, or **fine wrinkles on an organic model**. This allows artists to focus on the larger, more creative aspects of the model while letting the AI handle intricate, repetitive tasks.

For example, the AI could automatically apply a wrinkle pattern to a character's face based on the expression, or generate fine details of muscle fibers on a body model. The AI system analyzes the model's geometry and generates texture maps that align with natural patterns, making it faster to reach a polished look without the need for painstaking manual detailing.

Smart Mesh Generation

AI also aids in generating meshes that are more responsive to sculpting actions. By using algorithms that analyze the structure of a model in real-time, AI can predict where additional geometry should be added or removed, ensuring that the mesh behaves more naturally during sculpting. This can significantly reduce issues such as **topological stretching** or **polygonal pinching**, which often occur when working on more detailed or complex models.

Some AI systems even integrate with procedural sculpting tools, allowing for automatic corrections based on artistic guidelines. For instance, if a model starts to lose the intended proportions during sculpting, AI can provide suggestions or automatic adjustments to maintain the desired shape.

Automated Texturing and Style Transfer

Another promising use of AI in sculpting is **style transfer**, where AI can replicate the style of one 3D model and apply it to another. This is particularly useful for quickly adopting a specific artistic style across multiple projects. AI can learn textures, colors, and shading from an existing reference and then apply these characteristics to a new sculpture, saving time and effort in the texturing process.

Procedural Sculpting and Smart Materials

Procedural sculpting and the use of **smart materials** are revolutionizing the way digital models are created and textured. These techniques combine advanced algorithms and material libraries to generate assets in a more automated, yet highly customizable, way. Understanding these concepts allows you to push the limits of both your artistic vision and your productivity.

Procedural Sculpting: Efficiency Through Automation

Procedural sculpting involves creating models through mathematical algorithms that follow specific rules or patterns. Rather than manually manipulating every surface detail, you can set up rules that generate certain elements based on the base shape. For instance, a procedural sculpting technique can automatically generate a **rock surface** or **tree bark texture** based on a set of pre-established parameters.

In ZBrush, procedural sculpting can be used alongside **brush settings** and **alpha maps** to create complex textures or surfaces that would be incredibly time-consuming to generate manually. By adjusting the settings, you can create variations of patterns and designs quickly, providing a vast range of options with minimal effort.

Smart Materials for Dynamic Texturing

Smart materials are another cutting-edge tool that's transforming digital sculpting. These materials adapt to the shape, surface detail, and lighting of a model, changing dynamically based on the underlying geometry. For example, a smart material for **metal** might adjust its roughness, reflectivity, or gloss depending on the shape and curvature of the model, resulting in a more realistic and context-aware material application.

These materials are built with a set of rules that adjust their visual properties in response to changes in the model. For example, as you sculpt finer details into the surface, the material might add additional imperfections or dirt to match the new geometry. This makes them ideal for creating highly detailed, realistic models without the need for constant manual intervention.

Integration with Procedural Generators

One of the most advanced features of procedural sculpting is the ability to combine it with procedural texture generators. These generators can create textures that respond to the surface details of your model, adjusting in real-time as you sculpt. This integration can help produce complex organic structures like **rock formations**, **tree branches**, or **skin folds** with less effort, making it ideal for creating realistic environments or characters.

By combining procedural techniques with smart materials, digital artists can work more efficiently, making fewer manual adjustments and focusing more on high-level artistic decisions. The result is a much faster workflow that maintains high levels of detail and realism.

Portfolio Creation and Career-Level Presentation

In the competitive world of digital sculpting, your portfolio is the most important tool in showcasing your skills, experience, and creativity. A well-curated portfolio can be the difference between landing a dream project or being passed over in favor of another artist. As the digital art field continues to grow, understanding how to present your work in the best light is more critical than ever. This chapter provides insight into curating professional-level work for your portfolio, the best practices for both online and print portfolios, and how to build your personal brand as a digital sculptor.

How to Curate Professional Work

Curating your portfolio is not just about showcasing the best models or designs you've created. It's about presenting your abilities, your artistic vision, and your professionalism. To curate a portfolio that stands out, you need to be strategic about the work you display and the way you organize it.

Selecting Work for Your Portfolio

The first step in curating a professional portfolio is selecting the right pieces. You need to choose a range of work that showcases your versatility, attention to detail, and technical expertise. Aim for a balance of personal projects, client work (if applicable), and pieces that demonstrate your growth as an artist. Each piece should have a purpose and be there to highlight a particular skill or area of expertise.

Here are a few guidelines for selecting the work that should make the cut:

- **Quality over Quantity:** It's better to showcase fewer, highly refined pieces than to include every project you've worked on. Be selective. Your portfolio should demonstrate your best work and your ability to solve design problems creatively.

- **Diversity of Skills:** If possible, choose a variety of projects that display different skills. This could include character modeling, hard surface design, environments, texturing, or even stylized and realistic approaches. Highlight your ability to adapt to different styles, themes, and technical requirements.

- **Process and Progression:** Clients and employers are often as interested in your process as they are in the final product. Include a few pieces that show the progression of your work—from concept sketches to final renderings—to demonstrate how you approach the sculpting process, problem-solving, and refinement.

Avoid Overcrowding Your Portfolio

A common mistake is overcrowding your portfolio with too many pieces. Your portfolio should present your best work with clarity and simplicity. The goal is to give potential clients and employers an immediate sense of your abilities without overwhelming them. Each piece should be carefully chosen to convey a story about your skills, creativity, and artistic vision.

Additionally, make sure your portfolio is kept up to date. If you've been working on new skills, techniques, or projects, make sure those are reflected in your portfolio. An outdated portfolio can give the impression that you're not keeping up with industry trends or improving your craft.

Best Practices for Online and Print Portfolios

As digital sculpting becomes an increasingly competitive field, having a professional portfolio is essential, both online and in print. In the past, portfolios were traditionally printed in hard copies and shown in person, but today, the majority of portfolios are digital. Still, there are unique considerations when it comes to presenting your work in both formats.

Online Portfolios

In today's world, a strong online presence is critical. An online portfolio is your digital calling card, and it should be easy to navigate, fast to load, and mobile-friendly. Whether you use platforms like ArtStation, personal websites, or professional networks like LinkedIn, your online portfolio should be a showcase of your best work with a polished, professional feel.

Website Design and Navigation

Your website design should be simple and clean. Avoid cluttered layouts, and ensure that your work takes center stage. Navigation should be intuitive, and visitors should be able to find your work quickly. Categories or sections like "3D Models," "Concept Art," and "Texturing" can help organize your work and make it easier to navigate. A contact page should be readily available with an option for potential clients or employers to get in touch with you.

Image Quality

When uploading images to your online portfolio, make sure that they are high-quality and properly optimized. Use high-resolution images, but also ensure they don't load too slowly. Compress images without sacrificing detail so that visitors can view your work in all its glory without experiencing long loading times.

Showcase Process and Details

Consider including project breakdowns and making-of galleries in your online portfolio. These can include concept sketches, wireframes, and screenshots of the model at different stages of development. Such breakdowns give potential clients or employers insight into how you approach projects, problem-solving, and refinement. If applicable, add detailed descriptions of the work, the challenges you faced, and how you solved them.

Professional Bio and Social Links

Your portfolio should have a professional bio that highlights your background, skills, and experience. This helps potential employers or clients learn more about you. Be sure to include links to your professional social media accounts like LinkedIn or Twitter, where you can network and engage with the industry.

Print Portfolios

Although print portfolios are no longer as widely used as they once were, they are still relevant in certain situations, such as in-person interviews or client meetings. A print portfolio can give you a personal touch and allow you to stand out in a crowd.

Presentation and Layout

Your printed portfolio should be well-designed, with a simple layout that emphasizes your work. Use high-quality paper and prints to give the portfolio a professional feel. Keep the design minimal so that the artwork itself stands out. It's important to have a consistent style throughout the print portfolio, from the layout to the text used. A simple, elegant presentation will communicate professionalism and attention to detail.

Printed Materials to Include

While the printed portfolio should feature your best work, you should also include a few supplementary materials, such as a resume or business card, so that potential clients or employers have your contact details on hand. Depending on the nature of the portfolio, you may also include client testimonials, case studies, or brief descriptions of each project to provide context.

Building Your Brand as a Digital Sculptor

Building your personal brand as a digital sculptor is just as important as creating a great portfolio. Your brand is how others perceive you, and it encompasses everything from your portfolio to your online presence, social media activity, and reputation in the industry.

Define Your Artistic Identity

The first step in building a brand is defining your artistic identity. What sets you apart from other digital sculptors? Are you known for your realistic textures, stylized character designs, or hard surface modeling? Your portfolio and online presence should reflect the areas where you excel and the type of work you want to be hired for.

If you specialize in certain styles or types of projects (e.g., sci-fi characters, creature design, or environmental art), ensure your portfolio reflects that focus. This helps potential clients understand what you bring to the table and whether your skills align with their needs. It's crucial to market yourself authentically; trying to fit into a niche that isn't genuinely yours can undermine your brand's credibility.

Engage with the Community

To build a strong presence as a digital sculptor, engage with the larger artistic community. Share your work regularly on platforms like ArtStation, Instagram, or Behance, and be sure to interact with other artists, clients, and fans. Participate in online challenges or art contests to gain exposure and visibility. Engaging with your audience helps build your reputation and positions you as an active participant in the digital sculpting world.

Social media is a great platform to showcase your process, share tutorials, and interact with other professionals. Consider creating time-lapse videos of your sculpting process, offering tips on various techniques, or sharing behind-the-scenes glimpses of your work.

Networking and Building Professional Relationships

Networking is essential for career advancement. Attend industry events, both virtual and physical, such as conferences, webinars, and workshops. These events provide opportunities to connect with other digital artists, as well as potential clients and employers. Building these relationships can lead to collaborations, commissions, and job offers.

Additionally, collaborating with other artists can help you expand your portfolio and demonstrate your ability to work as part of a team. Showcase these collaborations in your portfolio to display your versatility and your capacity to work on diverse projects.

Consistency and Continuous Learning

Consistency is key to building a successful brand. Keep posting regularly, updating your portfolio, and engaging with your audience. Your brand should evolve over time, but it's important to stay consistent in the type of work you do and the way you present yourself.

As the digital sculpting industry continues to evolve, so too should your skills. Continuously learning and staying up to date with the latest software, tools, and techniques will keep you competitive. Attend workshops, take online courses, and always be open to experimenting with new methods. The more you learn, the more your brand will evolve into something dynamic and respected in the industry.

Topology Control and Edge Flow for Animation

A sculpted model with stunning detail can be rendered effectively in static scenes, but when that same model is needed for animation—whether for games, film, or real-time applications—its success is determined not just by form and texture, but by the quality of its topology. Topology, in this context, refers to the organization of polygons across the surface of a 3D model. The underlying edge flow, especially around areas of articulation like joints and facial muscles, must be constructed in a way that supports deformation without introducing unwanted stretching, compression, or artifacting.

Controlling topology effectively ensures that a model performs well when rigged, skinned, and animated. This chapter provides an advanced overview of manual retopology workflows in ZBrush, methods for designing edge loops that support deformation, the role of ZSphere retopology tools and the Topology Brush, and practical strategies for preparing sculpted characters for production-level animation.

Manual Retopology Workflows Inside ZBrush

Sculpting in ZBrush typically begins with high-resolution meshes created using tools like Dynamesh or Sculptris Pro. While these tools allow for rapid ideation and organic form creation, the resulting topology is rarely clean or organized enough for animation. This is where manual retopology becomes crucial. Retopology is the process of reconstructing the mesh with a focus on creating logical, optimized, and animation-ready edge flow.

Using ZRemesher as a Starting Point

ZRemesher is often the first tool used when preparing for manual retopology. While it's an automated process, ZRemesher is highly customizable. You can influence its output using guides, polygroups, and density targets. For example, using ZRemesher Guides, you can draw curves along the model to indicate the preferred direction of edge loops. These guides are especially helpful around joints such as shoulders, elbows, and knees, or around facial features like eyes and mouths.

Polygroups also play an important role. ZRemesher respects group borders and can generate cleaner topology transitions when each functional section of the model—such as limbs, torso, and head—is defined by its own group.

Even with well-placed guides and groups, ZRemesher's output often requires manual cleanup. For areas that need specific control—like the face or fingers—artists may opt to manually redraw the topology entirely.

Using ZModeler for Targeted Mesh Editing

Once ZRemesher has provided a working base mesh, the ZModeler brush becomes essential for further refinement. ZModeler offers low-level control over individual faces, edges, and points. It includes options to extrude, bridge, delete, insert edge loops, and more—all critical operations for correcting flow and maintaining quad-based structure.

One effective strategy is to isolate troublesome areas, such as the shoulder or groin, and use ZModeler to add or reflow edge loops to support bending. For instance, inserting extra edge loops near the joint can prevent geometry from collapsing during deformation.

ZModeler can also help clean up n-gons or triangles that may exist after the initial retopology. While quads are ideal, a well-placed triangle in a non-deforming area is sometimes acceptable, provided it doesn't impact surface continuity or rigging performance.

Projecting High-Resolution Detail

After completing the retopology, the new mesh is typically much lower in resolution than the original sculpt. To restore the details, the new mesh is subdivided progressively and projected onto the original using ZBrush's **Project**

All function. This projection should be performed gradually, checking for accuracy and errors at each subdivision level.

This workflow ensures that all the fine sculpted detail—wrinkles, pores, folds—is preserved while the model gains animation-ready topology.

Understanding Edge Loops for Deformation

The structural flow of polygons determines how a model behaves under deformation. In animation, particularly character animation, certain regions of the body bend and flex with more complexity than others. This necessitates the use of carefully placed **edge loops**—continuous chains of edges that form rings around the joints or muscle structures.

Edge Loop Fundamentals

Edge loops should follow the anatomical motion of the body. Around joints like elbows or knees, loops should be placed to mimic the folding of real skin. These loops act like creases or buffers, allowing the model to deform naturally without collapsing or stretching disproportionately.

Key regions where edge loops are critical include:

- **Eyes:** A minimum of four to five concentric loops should surround the eye socket. This allows for blinking, squinting, and directional gaze movement.

- **Mouth:** Proper lip movement requires loops that follow the contours of the lips, usually in an oval or circular form. These loops allow for expressions, speech, and secondary motion.

- **Shoulders and Elbows:** These joints benefit from multiple loop placements on both sides of the pivot point. This creates a hinge-like effect that supports flexion and extension.

- **Knees and Hips:** Similar to elbows, the legs require loops that can accommodate bending without introducing distortions.

Avoiding Common Topological Mistakes

Several topological issues can impede deformation:

- **Pinching:** This occurs when too many edges converge into a small area, causing visible artifacts when animated.

- **Stretching:** Insufficient geometry near bending areas leads to distorted or stretched textures and geometry.

- **Non-quad topology:** While not inherently problematic, triangles and n-gons often deform unpredictably. Keeping topology quad-based ensures better smoothing and rigging outcomes.

Using Flow to Guide Texture and Weight Painting

Good edge flow not only supports deformation but also benefits texturing and weight painting. Textures can stretch unnaturally across poorly constructed surfaces. When loops follow the contours of the surface, textures maintain their proportions more easily, and weights can be painted with more control and consistency.

Edge flow is also essential for blend shapes and morph targets. Clean loops enable localized deformation without affecting adjacent areas unnecessarily, ensuring that shape keys remain predictable and consistent.

Using ZSphere Topology Tools and Topology Brush

ZBrush offers specialized topology construction tools that go beyond traditional modeling. These tools allow artists to manually create topology directly over existing sculpts, giving full control over edge placement and structure.

ZSphere Retopology

ZSphere retopology is a method of wrapping a new mesh around an existing sculpt using a skeletal armature. Here's how the process works:

1. **Load the Original Sculpt** as a subtool.

2. **Create a ZSphere** as the new subtool.

3. **Activate Edit Topology Mode** under Tool > Rigging > Select Mesh and Tool > Topology > Edit Topology.

4. **Begin Drawing New Topology** over the original mesh. This is done by clicking to place new points and forming polygonal paths.

This approach allows you to control every vertex and edge loop manually. It's especially effective for heads, hands, or any area where precise topology is needed. Once complete, the topology can be converted into an adaptive skin and sculpted further or projected onto.

ZSphere-based retopology is slower than ZRemesher but provides more control and flexibility, particularly when preparing models for production pipelines where clean, predictable loops are essential.

Topology Brush Workflow

Another method for manually generating topology in ZBrush is the Topology Brush. This brush allows you to draw strokes directly on the model surface, and ZBrush will interpret these strokes as edges that define polygons.

Steps to use the Topology Brush:

1. Select the Topology Brush from the Brush palette.

2. Draw strokes on the surface where you want edge loops to exist.

3. Press **Enter** once the strokes are in place. ZBrush will convert the intersecting strokes into a new mesh with quads.

4. Use **Split Hidden** or **Extract** to separate this new mesh for further editing or sculpting.

The Topology Brush is excellent for creating local topology overlays, such as for the face, lips, or muscle loops. It's particularly useful for blocking out edge flows around eyes, mouth, or muscle creases where ZRemesher may struggle.

Preparing Sculpted Characters for Rigging and Animation

Once a sculpt has been retopologized and refined, it must be prepared for rigging and animation. This involves several technical and artistic considerations to ensure the model integrates well into a production pipeline and deforms reliably during performance.

Ensuring Uniform Topology Distribution

Rigging often requires the mesh to have relatively consistent density. Areas with overly dense topology next to low-density regions can produce problematic deformations or unexpected results during binding. It's important to even out the polygon distribution so that every joint or moving part is surrounded by an appropriate amount of geometry.

Even distribution does not mean all quads are the same size—some areas, like the face, still need higher resolution. But the transitions from high to low density should be smooth and calculated.

Naming Conventions and Group Management

For large production pipelines, models must be clean and organized. Each component—eyes, teeth, tongue, clothing—should be separate subtools or grouped accordingly. Use clear naming conventions and label polygroups logically. This makes it easier for riggers, animators, and technical artists to identify parts of the model during later stages.

Naming examples:

- "Body_LowRes"

- "Eyes_Inner"

- "Lashes_Top"

- "Tongue_Base"

Consistent organization prevents errors during skinning and ensures that assets are exportable and modular.

Creating UV Maps for Rigged Characters

For models intended for animation, UV mapping becomes essential, especially for texture artists and shader developers. ZBrush's UV Master plugin allows you to unwrap retopologized models quickly, but manual refinement is often required for complex meshes.

Best practices include:

- **Avoiding overlapping UVs** unless necessary (e.g., for mirrored textures).

- **Placing seams** in less visible areas (e.g., under arms or behind ears).

- **Maintaining consistent texel density**, especially across deforming areas like the face and hands.

A clean UV layout ensures that displacement, normal, and color maps render correctly and hold up during motion.

Exporting Models to External Programs

After all preparations are complete, the model must be exported in a format that supports external rigging and animation tools. **FBX** and **OBJ** are commonly used. FBX is preferred for rigs and baked animations, while OBJ works well for static geometry and UV-accurate exports.

Before export:

- **Freeze subdivision levels** or export the lowest and highest subdivisions separately.

- **Check normals** to ensure consistency across the mesh.

- **Apply proper scale** if the model is being used in a software like Maya or Blender where unit differences can cause import issues.

If the model is intended for game engines like Unreal Engine or Unity, polycount, material IDs, and UV layout must be optimized for performance. Clean edge loops are crucial in these environments to prevent shading errors during skeletal animation.

Morph Targets and Layer-Based Variations

Creating convincing and reusable deformations in a sculpting pipeline requires more than just static detailing. In professional production workflows—whether for animation, rigging, or concept iteration—sculptors must be able to store shape changes, revert to earlier stages, or blend deformations with absolute control. ZBrush provides robust functionality in the form of morph targets and sculpting layers, which allow artists to work non-destructively while developing dynamic forms such as facial expressions, pose changes, or progressive design variations.

This chapter covers the correct usage of morph targets, the Morph Brush for direct, localized control, the application of sculpting layers for storing facial expression variations, and the blending of morphs for seamless rigging and pose-based workflows. Together, these tools allow for a flexible sculpting experience without committing prematurely to changes or losing the original form.

Storing and Managing Morph Targets

Morph targets are snapshots of the current state of a model's geometry at a given subdivision level. In ZBrush, they serve as a reference that can be used to restore, compare, or blend between sculpted versions of a mesh. This functionality is particularly valuable when developing areas that undergo significant sculpting changes, such as during the creation of expression sets, corrective shapes, or alternative design directions.

Enabling Morph Targets

To store a morph target, the mesh must remain unaltered in terms of point order. That means you cannot delete or add geometry between storing and using a morph target—any change in vertex count or order will invalidate the saved state.

Steps to store a morph target:

1. Select the subtool you want to work on.

2. Go to **Tool > Morph Target**.

3. Click **StoreMT** (Store Morph Target) to record the current shape.

4. Sculpt freely, knowing you can revert to the stored version at any time.

If needed, click **Switch** to toggle between the stored target and the current sculpt. Clicking **DelMT** will remove the stored target and lock the morphing ability until a new target is stored.

Subdivision Levels and Morph Targets

Morph targets are stored at specific subdivision levels. If a morph target is stored at subdivision level 3, for example, it won't apply correctly at level 5 or 1. For best results, always return to the same subdivision level where the target was stored before activating morphing features.

Because morph targets are subdivision-specific, sculptors often store the target at the mid-level resolution where most forms are built. This provides a balance between detail and responsiveness when using tools like the Morph Brush.

Morph Target Use Cases

Common applications of morph targets include:

*   Restoring sculpted forms after making localized edits.

*   Isolating certain regions for rework while preserving surrounding detail.

- Comparing new sculpt changes with the original geometry.

- Creating accurate "before and after" states for corrective shapes.

- Preparing meshes for morph blending during animation rigging.

By maintaining a stored version of your sculpt, you gain a non-destructive safety net that allows experimentation without risking irreversible changes.

Using the Morph Brush for Reversible Edits

Once a morph target is stored, sculptors can take advantage of the **Morph Brush** to selectively restore parts of the original geometry. This brush compares the current sculpt to the stored morph target and blends between them, functioning similarly to an eraser or undo brush—but with greater nuance.

Accessing the Morph Brush

The Morph Brush is found in the Brush palette. It behaves like any standard sculpting brush but restores geometry toward the stored morph state rather than applying deformation.

Steps to use it:

1. Store a morph target as described previously.

2. Begin sculpting freely across the mesh.

3. Select the Morph Brush and begin brushing across areas you want to return to the original state.

Targeted Restoration

Unlike an undo operation, the Morph Brush works selectively. This is especially useful when you're happy with changes in one area but want to revert small regions to their original form. For example, you might be sculpting a new jawline and realize only the chin requires correction. Using the Morph Brush at low intensity, you can feather the blend between new and original geometry.

This local control is essential when working on symmetrical characters with asymmetrical edits, as it lets you restore one side without affecting the other. In production environments, it's frequently used to recover accidentally lost details, such as subtle wrinkles or overlapping skin forms.

Combining with Masking and Alphas

The Morph Brush can be combined with masking tools or alphas to isolate its effect even further. For instance:

- **Mask an area**, invert the mask, and use the Morph Brush to restore only the unmasked region.

- **Apply an alpha** to the Morph Brush to feather or pattern its influence.

This allows for highly precise control, whether you're dialing back muscle bulges, correcting facial expressions, or recovering lost surface detail without interrupting surrounding geometry.

Creating Facial Expression Sets with Layers

Layers in ZBrush allow you to store sculpting changes on top of a base mesh in an editable, non-destructive way. Unlike morph targets, which provide a snapshot of geometry at a moment in time, layers function as live recordings of changes applied to the mesh. They can be blended, muted, or deleted at will, making them ideal for sculpting facial expressions, pose variants, and alternate design iterations.

Understanding Layer Behavior

Each layer tracks sculpting changes from the moment it is created. Once a layer is active, any strokes you make are recorded to that layer, not baked into the base mesh. This makes it possible to:

- Create expressions such as smiles, frowns, squints, or blinks.

- Store alternate designs for facial anatomy or proportions.

- Build corrective shapes for rigging or blendshapes for animation.

To create a new layer:

1. Go to **Tool > Layers**.

2. Click **New Layer**. The layer becomes active.

3. Begin sculpting. All changes are recorded to this layer.

4. You can adjust the **Layer Intensity** slider to blend the effect.

5. Additional layers can be created for other expressions or variations.

Layer Naming and Management

Naming layers clearly is important in organized workflows, especially when building expression sets for rigging and animation. Use consistent labels such as:

- Smile_Left

- BrowRaise_Both

- Blink_Right

- Jaw_Open

You can then toggle layers on and off to preview combinations or isolate specific expressions for export.

Layers can be set to **Record**, **Inactive**, or **Playback Mode**:

- **Record**: The layer is capturing sculpting changes.

- **Inactive**: The layer remains present but no sculpting changes are applied to it.

- **Playback Mode**: You can blend or adjust intensity, but the layer cannot be edited directly.

Creating Corrective Poses or Shapes

For models that will undergo complex rigging or facial animation, layers can store corrective shapes that are triggered during specific poses. For example, a smile may cause the cheeks to bunch up—this bulge can be sculpted on a new layer and activated when the corresponding controller is triggered in the rig.

Because layers are editable and non-destructive, they allow for refinement over time. If a rigging artist requests an adjustment to the expression's volume or asymmetry, the sculptor can return to the layer and modify it without affecting the base mesh.

Blending Morphs for Rigging and Posing

One of the key reasons morph targets and layers are so valuable is their compatibility with external rigging workflows. Both can be exported as blend shapes (also called shape keys in some applications), which are essential for creating smooth, expressive animations in characters. Whether building facial rigs, joint-corrective shapes, or stylized transformations, the ability to blend morphs precisely is critical for professional-grade animation.

Exporting Blend Shapes from ZBrush

ZBrush supports the creation of morph shapes for external animation pipelines by exporting each shape as a separate OBJ or FBX file. These can be imported into rigging software like Maya or Blender and assigned as blend shapes or corrective morphs.

Steps to export blend shapes:

1. Create and store a morph target.

2. Sculpt the morph variation.

3. Export the modified mesh as an OBJ with a clear name (e.g., "Smile.obj").

4. Return to the morph target and switch to the original state.

5. Repeat the process for additional expressions.

These exported shapes should all share the exact same vertex count and point order. Most rigging software requires this to apply the morphs properly as deformation targets.

Using Blend Shapes for Facial Rigs

Once imported into a rigging tool, each morph can be driven by control curves, sliders, or custom attributes. This enables animators to create subtle facial expressions by blending multiple shapes—such as combining a brow raise with a slight smirk and an eye squint.

In many studios, a standardized set of expressions is used, such as the **FACS-based system** (Facial Action Coding System). This method categorizes facial expressions by muscle movement, and each action unit corresponds to a blend shape sculpted and exported from ZBrush.

ZBrush layers can be converted into separate meshes and exported, or you can use the Morph Target switching system for variations. Whichever method you choose, maintaining consistent naming and export order is key to integration.

Corrective Blend Shapes for Body Rigging

In addition to facial shapes, corrective morphs are often used for body rigging. These are secondary shapes that fix volume loss or distortion during extreme joint movements, such as:

- Elbow bend corrective bulge

- Shoulder lift deltoid expansion

- Hip twist asymmetry correction

The process for creating these is similar:

1. Pose the rig in an extreme position.

2. Export the posed model.

3. Sculpt the correction in ZBrush.

4. Export the corrected shape and apply it as a blend shape tied to the joint angle.

These corrective shapes can be blended automatically in the rig using driven keys or pose-based deformation systems.

Advanced ZModeler Techniques for Precision Modeling

The ZModeler Brush in ZBrush is often underestimated by artists who primarily focus on organic sculpting. However, it is a powerful polygon modeling system that, when mastered, unlocks precision workflows essential for architectural hard-surface work, mechanical structures, and low-poly base mesh generation. With careful application, ZModeler also integrates smoothly with traditional sculpting, allowing hybrid workflows that retain control over form and technical structure. This chapter explores advanced ZModeler features, including controlled extrusions, creasing, beveling, insertion techniques, modular asset creation, and the use of the Action Line for non-destructive adjustments.

Combining ZModeler with Traditional Sculpting

ZBrush is widely known for its organic sculpting strengths, yet its polygonal modeling tools—particularly the ZModeler Brush—allow for a hybrid approach where controlled geometry is used as a foundation before layering sculptural detail. Combining these two approaches gives the artist control over base topology while leveraging the expressive power of brush-based deformation.

Establishing the Base Mesh with ZModeler

ZModeler is particularly effective when a project requires structured geometry from the outset. Hard-surface forms such as helmets, armor, panels, and mechanical limbs benefit from starting with low-resolution quads laid out logically using ZModeler's tools.

For instance, you might block out a robotic chest plate by extruding panels from a cube, controlling edge loops with precision to maintain straight lines and planar faces. Once the basic form is complete, you can subdivide the mesh and switch to sculpting tools to add wear, tear, or ornamental details.

This workflow ensures that your sculpted details adhere to an underlying logical form, which is crucial when modeling anything that needs to be machined, assembled, or animated with clean deformations.

Dynamic Subdivision vs. Smoothing

ZModeler meshes often rely on **Dynamic Subdivision**, which visually smooths geometry without increasing the actual polycount. This makes it easier to preview how a model would look if subdivided while keeping the base mesh editable.

Artists can sculpt on a dynamically subdivided model, then return to polygon modeling for structural adjustments without losing resolution or introducing unnecessary subdivisions. This control is essential when building hybrid models that require both sculpted and modeled detail.

Edge Extrusions, Creasing, Bevels, and Inserts

Precision modeling in ZBrush relies heavily on understanding and properly executing edge-based modifications. ZModeler organizes actions by three target types: **Points**, **Edges**, and **Polygons**. Each of these has their own context menu of operations, such as extrusion, beveling, and insertion.

Edge Extrusion

Edge extrusion is one of the most fundamental tools in constructing models with complex topology. In ZModeler, extrusion is performed not just on polygons but also on individual edges. This is especially useful when modeling mechanical ribs, panels, and frames.

For example, to extrude an edge:

1. Hover over an edge with ZModeler selected.

2. Press Spacebar to bring up the Edge Action menu.

3. Choose **Extrude**, then select your desired behavior (single edge, multiple edges, edge loop).

4. Click and drag to execute the extrusion.

By holding down modifiers like Shift or Alt, you can further refine the extrusion axis and behavior, constraining it to the surface normal or world axis.

Edge extrusion is ideal for creating protrusions, lips, reinforcing structures, or mounting points, especially when working on components like brackets or armor sections.

Creasing for Subdivision Control

ZBrush handles creasing differently from many polygonal modelers. Creasing applies a sharp edge during subdivision without adding additional edge loops. This allows clean corner definition in low-resolution models while preserving editability.

To crease an edge:

1. Hover over the desired edge or edge loop.

2. Press Spacebar and select **Crease**.

3. Choose **Edge**, **Edge Loop**, or **All**.

4. Click to apply.

Once applied, the crease remains in effect until removed. This is helpful when using **Dynamic Subdivision**—creasing maintains shape integrity during visual smoothing without needing additional geometry.

Creases are essential for defining hard edges, such as the corners of a box, mechanical details, or even stylized forms like chiseled gemstone facets. They're particularly useful when the model will be exported for use in game engines or subdivided during rendering pipelines.

Beveling for Design Definition

Beveling edges softens transitions and introduces secondary design elements into a model. In ZModeler, beveling is achieved similarly to extrusion but provides chamfered geometry that can either stay flat or become rounded during subdivision.

To bevel an edge:

1. Hover over an edge.

2. Press Spacebar and choose **Bevel**.

3. Execute with a click and drag motion.

Beveling can be combined with creasing to maintain sharpness or allow for gentle smoothing in control loops. It's often used to define realistic wear edges or add style definition to parts like shoulder pads, hard armor, or stylized tech parts.

Bevel width and segment count can be adjusted in the ZModeler settings or interactively during the operation. For organic models, beveling adds nuance to transitions between surfaces; for hard surface work, it emphasizes construction realism.

Inserts and Interactive Poly Additions

ZModeler allows polygon inserts that dramatically increase flexibility when constructing modular designs. Artists can insert:

- **Edge Loops** (to control geometry flow or support subdivision)

- **Single Polygons** (for fill operations)

- **Complete Meshes** (with IMM brushes or Insert functions)

Using the **Insert Edge Loop** action, you can place additional loops with precision by adjusting parameters like multiple loop counts, equal spacing, or interactive placement. Insertions are especially useful when preparing geometry for animation or adding control edges near a crease.

Building Mechanical Structures and Modular Assets

Creating believable mechanical objects in ZBrush requires a structural approach. Unlike purely organic sculpts, mechanical parts are defined by engineered shapes, repeated units, and often symmetrical or mirrored components.

Planning Modular Forms

Before beginning sculpting or modeling, modular structures should be planned in terms of scale, repeatability, and alignment. ZModeler makes it easy to construct base forms with clean geometry that can be reused across a scene.

For example, building a set of mechanical pistons, armor plates, or ventilation components begins with low-resolution blocks. These are shaped using extrusion and bevels, creased as needed, then duplicated or mirrored to form consistent assemblies.

Using the **Transpose tool, Gizmo 3D**, or **ArrayMesh**, modules can be duplicated with control over spacing, rotation, and offset.

Creating Panel Breaks and Plating

One of the most powerful applications of ZModeler is in creating clean panel cuts and separations. Unlike organic brushes, which deform surfaces, ZModeler lets you physically separate geometry.

Common workflows include:

- Inserting edge loops around a form.

- Using **QMesh > PolyGroup All** to extrude panels outward or inward.

- Assigning different polygroups for visual separation.

- Using **Split > By Group** to break panels into subtools.

These paneling techniques are essential for robot parts, sci-fi armor, industrial surfaces, and mechanical assemblies. Combined with creasing and subdivision, they produce clean edge transitions and are ideal for baking into normal maps or exporting to game engines.

Sculpting Over ZModeler Meshes

Once mechanical parts are shaped, you can subdivide them and begin adding sculptural wear, scratches, and imperfections. ZBrush's **Trim**, **Slash**, and **Orb_Cracks** brushes are often used for this phase. Since the base topology is well-structured, sculpted details conform cleanly without introducing smoothing issues or structural distortion.

This dual-phase workflow—modeling for shape, sculpting for surface—ensures your assets retain both mechanical clarity and visual storytelling.

Working Non-Destructively with the Action Line

Precision modeling benefits from non-destructive transformations, especially when parts must be aligned, rotated, or scaled repeatedly. The **Action Line** in ZBrush—accessed via the Gizmo 3D or Transpose tools—enables this kind of manipulation without committing to irreversible transformations.

Understanding the Action Line

The Action Line is a visual guide consisting of three points:

- **Start Point**: The pivot origin.

- **Midpoint**: The directional axis.

- **End Point**: Used for scaling or measuring distances.

This tool can be aligned to specific parts of the model, reset to the world axis, or snapped to polygroups or vertices for precise alignment.

Common uses include:

- **Aligning parts** before merging or duplicating.

- **Scaling components** to match references or other assets.

- **Rotating arms, pistons, or joints** in modular assemblies.

- **Resetting object orientation** after using Deformation tools.

Unlike the standard Gizmo 3D manipulator, which acts globally, the Action Line allows operations relative to the selected geometry's orientation or surface normal. This is particularly useful when working with slanted components, radial symmetry, or tilted modules.

Symmetry and Local Transformations

ZModeler pairs well with symmetry tools. Symmetry in ZBrush can be used across X, Y, or Z axes and mirrored based on local or global object space. When combined with the Action Line, artists can perform accurate operations on mirrored components while retaining pivot independence.

You can also temporarily disable symmetry to work on asymmetrical parts, then re-enable it and mirror the modified geometry using **Mirror and Weld**, preserving consistent edge flow and structure.

Temporary and Reversible Positioning

The Action Line does not permanently alter the object's world-space pivot. You can rotate or reposition a module for alignment, sculpt detail or attach another object, then undo the transformation or reset it to its original position using **Transpose History** or undo stacks.

This non-destructive capability makes it ideal for:

- Creating hinge poses for sculpting

- Aligning subtools before Boolean operations

- Testing mechanical movement ranges

- Temporarily posing pieces without rigging

For artists working on modular kits, mechanical designs, or scenes with tight spatial requirements, this flexibility can save considerable time and reduce the need for external alignment tools.

Subdivision Strategies and Multiresolution Management

Subdivision is a fundamental concept in digital sculpting that governs how detail is added and managed across varying levels of mesh resolution. When used effectively, subdivision workflows provide sculptors with the flexibility to work broadly or precisely, allowing smooth transitions between blocking out forms and refining intricate surface details. For advanced users, managing subdivision levels becomes essential, particularly when working across complex subtools, modifying topology, or preparing models for animation and texture workflows.

This chapter explores how to sculpt efficiently between subdivision levels, preserve sculpted details through topological changes, reproject high-frequency data onto newly structured meshes, and manage multi-resolution models with stability and control across multiple subtools.

Working Between Subdivision Levels for Efficient Sculpting

Subdivision levels allow artists to switch between coarse and fine versions of their mesh while retaining control over overall form and detailed refinement. When properly managed, these levels serve as both creative and technical checkpoints during the sculpting process.

Understanding Subdivision in ZBrush

In ZBrush, subdivision does not occur automatically during sculpting. Instead, the artist initiates the process by using the **Divide** function, located under **Tool > Geometry**. Each time this function is used, the mesh is subdivided, quadrupling its polygon count while preserving the form of the original.

Subdivision levels are tracked within the tool, and artists can move up and down between them using the **Lower Res** and **Higher Res** buttons. This provides the ability to sculpt high-frequency detail on upper levels and make broad form adjustments at lower ones, without losing any data.

For example:

- At **Subdivision Level 1 or 2**, you adjust primary proportions, such as limb thickness or overall volume.

- At **Subdivision Level 5 or 6**, you refine pores, wrinkles, fabric textures, or engraving.

Switching between levels ensures non-destructive edits and provides an optimal sculpting experience that balances performance and precision.

Subdivision in Practice

When blocking out a character, begin at the lowest level possible. Focus on anatomical accuracy, gesture, and proportion before adding any detail. This allows you to sculpt with speed and control, without being distracted by surface complexity.

Only when the silhouette and underlying forms are complete should you begin subdividing. Each level of subdivision should correspond with a clear sculptural goal:

1. **Base Level**: Overall volume, silhouette

2. **Mid Level**: Muscle groups, anatomical transitions

3. **High Level**: Skin texture, tertiary details

Artists often toggle frequently between levels. For instance, if a cheekbone's structure feels too sharp while working at Level 5, returning to Level 2 or 3 allows for smoother, more natural adjustments, which will propagate cleanly upward.

This hierarchical approach mirrors traditional sculpting: coarse-to-fine, general-to-specific, structure-to-skin.

Preserving Details Across Topology Changes

In production workflows, a model's topology often changes after sculpting begins—whether through retopology, mesh optimization, or structural correction. These operations typically break the subdivision history, making it impossible to move between levels without reprojecting or transferring detail.

The Problem of Topology Breakage

Subdivision in ZBrush relies on consistent vertex order and count. If these change—even slightly—ZBrush no longer recognizes the mesh's subdivision structure. Common operations that cause this include:

- Merging subtools without careful geometry handling

- Retopologizing with ZRemesher or manual retopology

- Using Boolean operations

- Projecting without preserving topology

When this happens, you must rebuild subdivision levels and reproject details from the original sculpt. Preserving as much detail as possible during this transition requires specific preparation.

Before Retopology: Save and Duplicate

Before performing any operation that changes topology:

1. **Duplicate the subtool**: This will serve as the high-resolution detail source.

2. **Export the high-resolution mesh if needed**, in OBJ or FBX format for backup.

3. **Retopologize or alter topology** on the duplicated mesh.

Once a new base mesh has been created, you can subdivide it incrementally and project the details from the original.

This ensures that, even if the topology shifts, your sculpted information is recoverable and transferable.

Preserving Sculpted Features

When reconstructing subdivision levels, it's essential to match the overall form as closely as possible before projection. The base mesh must sit within the volume of the original, or projection artifacts will appear—such as surface spikes, distortions, or mismatched edges.

To avoid this:

- Use **ZRemesher with symmetry and guides** to retain silhouette.

- Rebuild subdivision levels gradually: subdivide the new mesh one level at a time.

- Keep the original visible during projection for constant reference.

Reprojecting Details After Retopology

ZBrush offers a robust projection system that allows sculptors to transfer high-resolution detail from one mesh to another—even when topology and vertex count differ. This capability is key for recovering surface features after retopology or rebuilding subdivision levels.

Using Project All

The **Project All** function under **Tool > SubTool** is the primary method for transferring details:

1. Subdivide the new mesh to match or exceed the polygon density of the original sculpt.

2. Select the new mesh as the active subtool.

3. Make the original high-resolution sculpt visible (but not active).

4. Click **Project All**.

ZBrush will project the visible subtool's details onto the current one. Adjust **Distance**, **PA Blur**, and **PA Inflate** sliders to fine-tune projection strength and behavior.

Repeat the projection at each subdivision level to gradually capture increasing detail. This staged projection ensures clean surface transfer without distortion.

Using the Project Brush for Targeted Transfer

If **Project All** introduces errors in specific areas, the **Project Brush** can be used instead. This brush allows for selective detail transfer by manually brushing one mesh onto another:

1. Position the new mesh over the original.

2. Select the Project Brush.

3. Carefully paint over the target area to transfer detail.

This method is useful for isolated regions such as eyelids, fingers, or tightly packed areas where automatic projection may fail.

Best Practices for Clean Projection

To maximize accuracy:

- Match the mesh density as closely as possible.

- Avoid extreme differences in topology layout between source and target.

- Manually smooth projection artifacts using the **Smooth**, **Trim**, or **Polish** brushes post-projection.

- Mask sensitive regions before projection if you want to preserve the new mesh's structure there (such as around eyes or joints).

When done correctly, projected meshes are visually indistinguishable from the original sculpt and ready for UV unwrapping, baking, or animation rigging.

Multi-Resolution Sculpting Across Complex Subtools

Advanced characters and scenes often consist of multiple subtools, each with different subdivision levels. Efficiently managing these subtools is essential for performance, organization, and iterative workflow.

Subdivision Level Matching

Subtools must be handled individually in terms of their subdivision hierarchy. A common challenge is synchronizing the subdivision levels of multiple parts—like head, torso, hands, and clothing—so that they can be sculpted in harmony.

For example:

- A face might require six subdivision levels to hold pore-level detail.

- A shirt may only require four levels to maintain textile fold quality.

- An armor plate may never be subdivided beyond level three if sculpted ornamentation is limited.

To maintain performance, only subdivide subtools as needed. Avoid pushing all subtools to the same high level unless detail demands it.

When working across subtools:

- Use **Solo mode** to focus on one part without performance penalties.

- Organize subtools logically (e.g., Body > Clothing > Armor > Accessories).

- Apply subdivision only where sculpting or baking demands it.

Working with Shared Detail Standards

For consistency, especially in production settings, maintain a consistent **detail resolution** across subtools that will be viewed closely or rendered together.

For instance, if the face has pore detail, hands and neck should match in fidelity to avoid rendering mismatches. Disparities become evident under lighting or when applying shared material shaders.

To standardize:

- Use the **Polyskin display** to check density visually.

- Ensure UV tiles or texel density align proportionally.

- Reproject detail from reference subtools if needed to synchronize resolution.

Subtool Performance Management

When managing dozens of subtools, subdivision becomes a major performance factor. To optimize workflow:

- **Disable higher subdivision levels** on inactive subtools.

- Use **Lower Subdiv** before saving heavy projects.

- Use **Decimation Master** for subtools that won't require further sculpting.

- Merge temporarily with **Merge Down**, then separate again to reduce project load.

Complex models—such as characters with gear, props, and base mesh—can reach hundreds of millions of polygons across all subtools. Careful management of subdivision and projection ensures sculpting remains responsive and stable.

Vector Displacement Workflows

The development of detailed, three-dimensional surface features is an essential aspect of modern digital sculpting. For professionals working across concept design, visual effects, and interactive media, traditional height-based displacements often fall short in capturing the depth and dimensional complexity of intricate sculptural work. Vector displacement maps (VDMs) solve this limitation by allowing multi-directional displacement—including overhangs, folds, and undercuts—thereby preserving full sculptural form. This chapter explores the creation of VDMs in ZBrush, the technical distinction between height and vector displacement, the baking process for third-party rendering engines, and targeted use cases in stylized character creation and creature-based modeling.

Creating and Applying 3D Displacement Brushes

Vector displacement brushes in ZBrush allow artists to sculpt with pre-defined, three-dimensional patterns. Unlike alphas or standard displacement, VDM brushes embed directional information, enabling forms to project out from and below the surface in ways heightmaps cannot replicate.

Establishing a Clean Base Mesh for VDM Extraction

To create a reliable VDM brush, the source mesh must be constructed with clarity and minimal noise. The brush form is typically sculpted on a subdivided plane or low-poly cube, subdivided evenly across its surface.

Key considerations:

- Use a **high-resolution square plane** with even quads to avoid distortion.

- The detail should emerge **perpendicularly from the plane**, to ensure predictable application.

- Avoid excessive overhangs that stretch beyond the vector range ZBrush can capture.

- Reset transformations and center the model before extraction.

Sculpting the Brush Form

The form you sculpt will determine how the VDM behaves. For best results:

- Use **Clay**, **DamStandard**, and **Move** brushes to sculpt organic folds or creases.

- Consider where negative space exists, as VDMs can handle depth that would break a heightmap.

- Minimize stretching by keeping deformations proportional to the plane's resolution.

After the form is complete, mask the area to extract or define the brush region. The **Create MultiAlpha Brush** function can also be used for sets of VDMs stored as a brush library.

Creating the Vector Displacement Map Brush

Once the detail is ready:

1. Go to **Brush > Create > Create VDM from Mesh**.

2. ZBrush captures the vector offset of each vertex from the plane and stores it as a multichannel displacement.

3. A new brush appears in your tool menu, now capable of stamping the sculpted form onto any surface.

This brush behaves like a sculpting stamp but preserves volume, overhangs, and recesses—far beyond what a 2D alpha could achieve.

Editing and Controlling VDM Brushes

After creation, the VDM brush can be further edited:

- Adjust the **intensity** under the Brush > Modifiers panel.

- Rotate or flip the vector data using **Stroke settings**.

- Use **Lazy Mouse** for smoother application paths.

When used with symmetry, radial stroke, or drag-rect, these brushes can rapidly populate surfaces with anatomical features, mechanical parts, or stylized motifs.

Difference Between Height and Vector Displacement

Understanding the difference between standard height-based displacement and vector displacement is essential when choosing which to use in a given context. While both serve the purpose of simulating surface detail beyond the polygonal resolution, their technical behavior and visual impact differ significantly.

Height Displacement Maps

A traditional displacement map stores scalar data in a grayscale image, where white values represent maximum elevation and black values represent maximum depression. This is known as **height-based displacement**.

Characteristics:

- Operates **along surface normals**.

- Cannot represent folds, overhangs, or hooked forms.

- Typically stored as a single-channel 16-bit or 32-bit image (e.g., EXR, TIFF, or PNG).

- Best suited for subtle surface detail like pores, wrinkles, or brickwork.

Limitations:

- Fails to represent any geometry that bends outward or projects back under itself.

- Edge detail flattens or clips when pushed beyond certain amplitude levels.

- Causes unnatural shading when attempting to mimic undercut surfaces.

Vector Displacement Maps

Vector displacement stores directional data for each point on a surface. Instead of a scalar elevation, it stores a **3D vector** that describes how far and in which direction a vertex should be displaced. This allows for multi-directional deformation from the original base mesh.

Characteristics:

- Encoded as a **three-channel RGB image**, with each channel representing X, Y, and Z displacement.

- Capable of generating fully volumetric features, including horns, sockets, and cavities.

- Interpreted by render engines as full 3D vector transformations, not surface-normal offsets.

- Ideal for modular sculpting, reusable details, and physically accurate displacement.

Limitations:

- Requires compatible rendering engines and correct interpretation of tangent space.

- Can introduce render artifacts if improperly baked or applied to poorly mapped geometry.

- Not ideal for subtle surface textures, where grayscale displacement is more efficient.

In practice, both maps can be used together—height maps for micro-detail and vector displacement for structural sculptural data.

Baking Vector Maps for External Renderers

To export vector displacement data for use in external render engines (such as Arnold, V-Ray, or Blender's Cycles), a precise workflow is necessary to ensure the maps render correctly.

Preparing the Mesh

Before baking:

1. Ensure that the low-resolution base mesh has clean topology and UVs. Vector displacement requires accurate UV mapping to avoid direction distortion.

2. The high-resolution sculpt must align perfectly with the low-resolution mesh in 3D space.

3. Apply morph targets if needed to maintain shape consistency between high and low meshes.

Using Multi Map Exporter

ZBrush provides a plugin called **Multi Map Exporter** that simplifies the process of generating displacement and vector maps.

Steps:

1. Go to **ZPlugin > Multi Map Exporter**.

2. Select the subtool and check **Vector Displacement Map** (VDM).

3. Choose your desired file format (EXR or TIFF recommended).

4. Under **Export Options**, set the tangent space, mid-value, and scale to match your rendering engine's specifications.

5. Click **Create All Maps**.

Settings Overview:

- **Mid Value**: Defines the zero-displacement point. Typically 0.5 for EXR/TIFF maps.

- **Scale**: Adjusts how strongly the displacement will be interpreted.

- **Flip Channels**: Depending on the renderer, you may need to flip R, G, or B to match the tangent basis.

Integrating in External Render Engines

Each render engine interprets vector maps differently. Below are generalized requirements:

- **Arnold (Maya)**: Use **aiVectorDisplacement** node. Set mode to **Tangent** and connect RGB map to vector displacement slot.

- **V-Ray**: Use **VRayDisplacementMod** with vector displacement enabled. Load the RGB EXR map and enable Tangent setting.

- **Cycles (Blender)**: Connect image texture to **Vector Displacement** node. Input needs tangent space, and mesh must have UVs and normals.

Common Troubleshooting Tips:

- If geometry explodes on render: mid-value is incorrect or UVs are distorted.

- If detail appears reversed: flip appropriate vector channels or adjust tangent space.

- If displacement appears flat: increase map scale or check render subdivision settings.

Use Cases for Stylized and Creature-Based Sculpts

Vector displacement is especially effective for workflows involving stylized characters and complex creature designs, where exaggerated forms or nested volumes are critical to the design aesthetic. In such workflows, traditional displacement often results in surface clipping or artifacts. VDMs preserve depth, silhouette complexity, and stylized exaggeration.

Stylized Characters with Patterned Form

In stylized modeling, exaggeration of volumes—such as puffed cheeks, exaggerated folds, or bulbous features—is often required. Standard displacement flattens these forms or forces topology to accommodate higher resolution.

Using VDMs, stylized details like engraved curls, stylized foliage, or ornamental hair tufts can be stamped efficiently across the surface, retaining three-dimensional shape and volume.

For instance:

- **Fantasy armor** may incorporate leaf-like ridges that fold and undercut into the plating.

- **Clothing details** such as layered embroidery, stylized buttons, or magical runes can be applied using vector displacement stamps.

- **Hair tufts** or horn ridges can be inserted rapidly with a custom VDM brush, eliminating the need for manual retopology.

Creature Design and Anatomical Detailing

Creature modeling often involves complex surface details such as overlapping scales, gills, horns, or layered membranes. These features frequently possess undercut geometry or radial deformation that cannot be replicated with traditional height maps.

VDMs are especially useful for:

- **Scales that wrap around limbs** and follow muscle direction.

- **Spines and barbs** that grow from the surface at complex angles.

- **Branching tissue structures** such as tendrils, whiskers, or antennae that bend away from the model's surface.

Because VDMs allow forms to emerge or wrap in multiple directions, they enable anatomically accurate surface modeling without sacrificing base mesh integrity. This is critical for animatable assets where topology must remain clean and predictable.

Reusable Modular Sculpting

VDM libraries can be created and reused across multiple projects. An artist might maintain a brush set containing:

- Stylized leaf curls

- Scale patterns in different sizes

- Horn tips or claw sockets

- Repeating ornamental symbols

By using these as brush stamps, the artist maintains stylistic consistency across a creature or character lineup, accelerates production time, and avoids the need for manual duplication of complex forms.

Each VDM brush behaves as a mesh micro-insert with three-dimensional fidelity, allowing for hybrid workflows between traditional modeling and high-frequency sculpting.

FiberMesh for Advanced Hair and Fur Creation

FiberMesh offers an integrated solution in ZBrush for creating complex strand-based systems such as hair, fur, feathers, and grass with sculptable precision. Unlike texture-based hair maps or baked normal effects, FiberMesh generates physical geometry that responds to lighting, shadow, and deformation in a realistic manner. This makes it especially valuable in workflows where visual fidelity and surface interaction are critical—whether for stylized characters, creature design, or detailed product visualization.

In this chapter, we will examine how to sculpt with FiberMesh using procedural settings, manage and groom the resulting fibers, convert them into usable geometry, and export strand-based structures for further development in external rendering and simulation platforms.

Sculpting with FiberMesh Settings

FiberMesh generates fibers from the surface of a mesh using a procedural system that defines length, width, taper, gravity, and variation per strand. These fibers are not painted textures or illusions—they are three-dimensional strands extruded and controlled through parameter-based generation.

Activating FiberMesh

To begin working with FiberMesh:

1. Select the subtool or area where fibers will grow.

2. Mask the target area (or invert a mask to isolate).

3. Navigate to **Tool > FiberMesh > Preview**.

4. Toggle **Preview** on to generate the fibers.

The preview is non-destructive until you accept the result, meaning you can adjust parameters and instantly see the effect without modifying the original subtool.

FiberMesh Parameter Groups

Several categories of settings control the behavior of the fibers:

- **Coverage**: Defines the percentage of masked area to emit fibers.

- **Length**: Controls how long each fiber grows from the surface.

- **Segments**: Determines the number of divisions per strand, affecting flexibility and smoothness.

- **Profile**: Sets the number of sides around each fiber, similar to radial segments on a cylinder.

- **Taper**: Controls how the fiber narrows toward the tip.

- **Gravity and Clump**: Simulate real-world physical influences, adding natural sag and bundling.

- **Color**: Fibers can inherit surface color or be assigned a random or gradient palette.

For short, dense fur (such as on mammals), use high coverage, short length, low taper, and minor gravity. For long, stylized hair, increase segment count, taper, and enable clumping for layered behavior.

All of these settings can be randomized or varied per strand, allowing for a highly organic result. Artists can store multiple FiberMesh presets to create reusable configurations for different material types—fur, grass, feathers, or synthetic fibers.

Accepting and Editing Fibers

Once the desired configuration is previewed:

1. Click **Accept** to generate FiberMesh as a new subtool.

2. The fibers are now editable as sculptable geometry with their own subdivision levels and masking.

FiberMesh objects behave like any other subtool. You can sculpt them, split sections, or reassign polygroups. However, due to their complexity and potential polygon count, they may need to be managed carefully to preserve performance.

Styling and Grooming Techniques

Styling FiberMesh requires a blend of sculpting intuition and technical control. After fiber generation, a wide array of grooming brushes becomes available to manipulate direction, volume, and pattern.

Grooming Brush Types

ZBrush includes several grooming brushes designed for FiberMesh:

- **GroomHairLong**: Ideal for long strand sweeping and length adjustments.

- **GroomTurbulence**: Adds noise and randomness for natural motion.

- **GroomBlow**: Simulates wind or directional force across strands.

- **GroomSpike**: Sharpens and raises clumps to create stylized looks.

- **GroomClumps**: Groups strands together based on local proximity.

- **GroomStrong**: Provides maximum force for reshaping dense areas.

These brushes affect only FiberMesh strands. To activate them, select a grooming brush from the Brush palette while the FiberMesh subtool is active.

Polygroups and Masking for Local Styling

Fibers are automatically assigned polygroups by strand root. This allows for group-based masking and grooming.

Workflow example:

1. Use **Ctrl + Shift + Click** to isolate a group of fibers.

2. Apply grooming only to this section (e.g., a beard, a mohawk).

3. Repeat for other groups to create layered hair styles.

Artists can also apply **Masking** to protect sections of the fiber while adjusting others, such as locking the base of the hair while adjusting tips.

Controlling Strand Direction and Flow

For controlled directionality:

- Use **Move Topological** to reshape large fiber groups.

- Use **Smooth** to reduce chaotic or tangled strands.

- Apply **Trim Dynamic** or **HPolish** to flatten areas for parted styles.

Combining brushes in sequence creates complex layering, such as base grooming with GroomHairLong, followed by volume shaping with GroomClumps, and final noise application with GroomTurbulence.

Converting FiberMesh to Geometry

While FiberMesh strands are real geometry, they can be further processed for optimization, detailing, or export. In some workflows, artists may need to simplify strands, flatten them for baking, or prepare them for export to engines that do not support raw strand data.

Converting to Thick Geometry

FiberMesh strands are initially tubular, based on their profile setting. This profile can be increased to give volume, but can also be reduced to flat ribbons for stylization.

Steps to control thickness:

- In **Tool > FiberMesh > Modifiers**, adjust the **Profile** slider to change cross-section.

- Lower profiles (1–2) produce ribbon-like hair.

- Higher profiles (6–12) create tube-like fur or thick braids.

To finalize as static geometry:

1. Use **Delete Lower** to remove subdivision levels.

2. Apply **DynaMesh** to remesh and fuse fibers.

3. Use **ZRemesher** if needed for animation-ready topology.

Simplifying Fibers for Baking or Sculpting

In cases where hair is not needed as actual strands (e.g., low-poly characters, game assets), FiberMesh can be baked into displacement or normal maps.

Workflow:

- Convert FiberMesh to a high-resolution mesh.

- Place it above a low-resolution scalp or body mesh.

- Use **Project All** or normal map baking tools to imprint detail onto the base mesh.

This method is common for eyebrows, body stubble, or stylized hair patterns, where geometry complexity must be minimized.

Exporting Hair Systems to Other Software

For integration into external pipelines—such as animation, simulation, or real-time rendering—FiberMesh must be exported in a format that supports strand interpretation or as usable polygonal proxies.

FBX Export for Geometry-Based Workflows

If the receiving software uses polygon hair (e.g., game engines, low-poly animation), export the FiberMesh subtool as a mesh.

Steps:

1. Select FiberMesh subtool.

2. Go to **ZPlugin > FBX ExportImport**.

3. Choose **Export SubTool** and set file format to FBX.

4. Confirm scale and axis settings depending on the target application (e.g., Y-Up for Maya, Z-Up for Blender).

The exported file includes strand geometry, UVs (if applied), and color information if polypaint is used.

Alembic or Curve Export Workaround

ZBrush does not natively export strands as curve primitives or Alembic hair caches. However, several workarounds exist:

- **Convert Fibers to ZCurves** using scripting tools (community plugins).

- **Export as low-profile ribbon geometry** and convert to guides in another program.

- **Use intermediate software (e.g., Maya, Blender)** to interpret strands as curves.

For Blender:

- Import FiberMesh geometry.

- Use modifiers (such as "Skin" or "Curve to Mesh") to convert geometry back to curves.

- Reassign strand data and run particle simulation if needed.

For Maya:

- Import FBX geometry.

- Use **NURBS conversion** or **XGen** guide creation to reconstruct hair guides from FiberMesh strands.

- Apply modifiers to style and simulate using native tools.

Rendering Considerations

FiberMesh strands render well in ZBrush's BPR system. However, for production renders, consider converting strands into guides for hair systems such as:

- **XGen** in Maya

- **Hair and Fur** in 3ds Max

- **Particle Hair** in Blender

- **Yeti** or **Ornatrix** for high-end control

In these systems, converted FiberMesh strands can drive render hair, allowing dynamic simulation, lighting-based transparency, and strand-level shading. Assign materials based on strand color, root-to-tip gradient, or randomized variation.

Exporting with Texture and Color Data

FiberMesh can inherit vertex color from the underlying mesh. This color is retained in the **polypaint** data and can be exported with the mesh using **FBX ExportImport**.

To use this in external renderers:

- Export mesh with polypaint enabled.

- In the receiving software, use vertex color input in shader to modulate strand color.

- Alternatively, bake polypaint to texture and assign as root-tip gradient.

Color transfer is particularly useful for animal fur, beards, or stylized characters where strand tone plays an important role in visual fidelity.

Spotlight Pro for Texture Projection and Painting

Spotlight Pro is a sophisticated texture projection tool integrated within ZBrush that enables artists to precisely project images directly onto their digital sculpts. Unlike conventional painting methods, Spotlight Pro allows detailed control over texture placement, scale, rotation, and opacity, making it invaluable for tasks ranging from photo-realistic texturing to applying precise decals on hard-surface models. Its strength lies in the ability to quickly blend photographic reference textures onto intricate models, reducing the need for external texturing applications.

This chapter explores advanced techniques for loading and manipulating reference images using Spotlight, painting textures directly onto sculpted surfaces, applying decals accurately to hard-surface geometry, and effectively managing projection distortion and blending for realistic results.

Loading and Adjusting References with Spotlight

Spotlight begins with loading images as references or textures into ZBrush. Proper preparation and manipulation of these images directly impact the quality and accuracy of texture projection.

Preparing Images for Spotlight

Before importing images into Spotlight, it's crucial to ensure optimal quality and resolution. Textures should ideally have uniform lighting, minimal shadowing, and sufficient resolution to maintain detail when projected onto your sculpt. Images in formats such as PNG, TIFF, or JPEG are compatible and provide clear, sharp detail. Large images (2K to 4K resolution or higher) are recommended to capture finer details such as skin pores, fabric weave, or mechanical surface imperfections.

Activating Spotlight and Image Loading

To begin:

1. Open the Texture Palette and import the desired images.

2. Select your imported image, then click the "Add to Spotlight" button, found within the Texture Palette interface. This action places the image onto the Spotlight canvas.

3. Activate Spotlight mode by pressing the "Z" key, displaying a dial that includes numerous manipulation tools for image adjustment.

Spotlight's control wheel provides interactive tools such as Scale, Rotate, Move, Opacity adjustment, and Hue/Saturation control. You can cycle through images or add multiple references simultaneously by repeating the import and loading process.

Adjusting and Organizing Spotlight References

Proper adjustment of your Spotlight images is fundamental for efficient workflow:

- **Scaling and Placement:**
  Click and drag on the Spotlight's Scale handle to adjust your image size. Move the images strategically near the region of the model you intend to texture. Effective placement ensures minimal distortion and accurate texture alignment.

- **Rotation and Alignment:**
  Rotate images by dragging the rotation handle, aligning directional details like fabric fibers or skin patterns accurately with the model surface. For symmetrical models, mirror images by flipping horizontally or vertically to match anatomical symmetry.

- **Opacity and Transparency:**
  Adjust opacity using Spotlight's dial to allow visual blending and proper

alignment of textures with underlying geometry. Reduced opacity helps visualize how textures overlay complex sculptural forms before committing paint strokes.

- **Color Adjustments:**
  Utilize Spotlight's built-in Hue, Saturation, and Intensity controls to match your reference texture color tones with the existing palette of your sculpt. This facilitates seamless color integration when painting.

- **Organizing Multiple Images:**
  When using several references simultaneously, position each clearly on the Spotlight canvas. Arrange related images closely together—for instance, different angles of a single object or complementary textures like rust and metal—to streamline painting processes.

Painting Textures Directly onto Sculpts

Spotlight excels at transferring detailed textures onto models, offering control over how photographic reference images translate into sculpted detail.

Activating Polypaint and Preparing the Model

Before painting:

1. Select your sculpted subtool and ensure adequate polygon resolution, as polypaint relies on vertex count for detail clarity.

2. Activate Polypaint by clicking "Colorize" in the Polypaint menu. Assign a neutral white or base color to your model to accurately observe transferred textures.

Texture Projection Workflow

To project texture from Spotlight onto your model:

1. Position the Spotlight image over the model area targeted for texturing.

2. Enter Projection mode by pressing the "Z" key, hiding Spotlight's dial and making images non-interactive but paintable.

3. Select a standard brush with RGB mode activated. Adjust RGB intensity based on desired transparency and blending strength.

4. Begin painting directly onto the mesh. ZBrush will project image details onto the surface where the brush is applied, capturing color, pattern, and detail precisely.

Layering and Blending Textures

For depth and realism, layering textures is crucial:

- First, apply a base texture layer at full RGB strength.

- Lower RGB intensity gradually and overlay secondary textures to introduce complexity and variation. For instance, project subtle skin blemishes, dirt, or fabric textures over initial passes.

- Use the Smooth brush at low intensity to blend transitions between textured areas, eliminating harsh edges and achieving a natural integration.

By methodically building layers, complex surface textures such as aged skin, weathered metals, or layered paint effects can be realistically rendered.

Using Spotlight for Hard Surface Decals

Applying decals—such as logos, symbols, text, or detailed graphics—is common in industrial design, sci-fi modeling, and mechanical assets. Spotlight's precise control makes this process straightforward and efficient.

Preparing Decals for Spotlight

High-quality, transparent-background PNGs are recommended. Decals should have clear edges and a high pixel resolution to maintain sharpness upon projection. Ensure the image background is transparent or a solid color that can easily be keyed out using Spotlight's color intensity controls.

Projecting Decals onto Hard Surfaces

1. Position your decal precisely over the intended location on the hard-surface model. Scale and rotate it accurately to match the surface orientation and size requirements.

2. Adjust the opacity to preview decal placement before committing to projection.

3. Use the DragRect stroke type for precise, one-click projection, or carefully paint with standard strokes for manual placement and finer control.

4. Upon projection, verify decal alignment from multiple angles, ensuring accurate visual integration.

Creating Realistic Decal Integration

Decals placed directly can appear unnaturally sharp. For realistic integration:

- Reduce RGB intensity slightly during projection to simulate partial paint wear.

- Overlay subtle texture maps such as scratches or grime using low-opacity painting passes to embed decals convincingly into the surface.

- Carefully smooth or erase decal edges where they meet seams, curves, or transitions, enhancing realism and visual authenticity.

Managing Projection Distortion and Blending

One challenge in texture projection is managing distortion, especially on complex geometry or irregularly curved surfaces. Effective blending ensures textures look seamless, organic, and consistent from all viewing angles.

Identifying and Preventing Projection Distortion

Distortion commonly occurs where projection angles are extreme or mesh geometry is dense and irregular:

- **Projection Angle:**
  Always project textures directly perpendicular to the surface where possible. Angled projections stretch and distort details. Regularly reposition the Spotlight reference image to match surface normals closely.

- **Surface Curvature and Density:**
  High-density meshes hold detail better but may show unexpected distortions in tightly curved areas. Simplify initial projections on complex areas by using smaller, incremental painting passes.

Corrective Techniques for Distortion

When distortion occurs:

- Use the Morph brush or Smooth brush gently to relax stretched polygons and reduce visible texture distortion after projection.

- Project again from a different angle, blending the corrected areas softly into previously projected textures.

- In severe cases, adjust Spotlight images with distortion deliberately applied in image editing software beforehand, compensating for expected projection deformation.

Advanced Blending Strategies

Seamless integration of projected textures involves strategic blending:

- Use a low RGB intensity brush to softly blend projected textures into untextured areas, creating natural fade-outs.

- Apply selective Gaussian blur or softening to Spotlight images before projection to facilitate smoother blending transitions, especially for organic textures.

- Mix manual polypainting alongside Spotlight projections, filling minor gaps or refining subtle details that automated projection may miss.

Projection with Masks and Alphas

Masks and alphas enhance projection control:

- Mask sensitive or finished regions before projection to protect details from unintended overpainting.

- Apply alpha brushes during projection for complex edge effects—such as chipped paint, rust patches, or wear patterns—to seamlessly blend textures with existing surfaces.

- Alphas combined with Spotlight projections create realistic aging or damage effects rapidly without extensive manual painting.

Efficient Workflow Recommendations

For optimized workflow and quality outcomes:

- Work incrementally, projecting smaller, manageable sections sequentially rather than one large image at once.

- Regularly assess your model from multiple perspectives during projection to detect early signs of distortion or unnatural blending.

- Keep Spotlight's interactive dial hidden (press Z) during painting passes to maintain maximum viewport clarity and accurate texture application.

Spotlight Pro thus becomes not just a projection tool, but a comprehensive painting solution capable of producing intricate texture results swiftly and accurately, significantly enhancing productivity across complex sculpting and texturing pipelines.

ZSketch and Advanced ZSphere Armature Techniques

ZBrush offers versatile tools for sculptors who wish to approach digital modeling using methods similar to traditional clay sculpting. Among these, ZSketch and ZSphere armature techniques stand out by providing flexible frameworks that facilitate rapid ideation and detailed anatomical study. ZSpheres function effectively as internal skeletons or armatures, supporting the structure of complex models, while ZSketch adds volume directly onto these skeletal forms. These techniques enable artists to explore organic shapes intuitively, facilitating anatomical accuracy, rapid form iteration, and dynamic posing early in the modeling process.

This chapter details comprehensive workflows involving ZSpheres as anatomical armatures, direct volume creation with ZSketch brushes, converting ZSketch forms into usable base meshes, and utilizing adaptive skinning techniques for dynamic posing and flexible character design.

Using ZSpheres as Anatomical Skeletons

ZSpheres are foundational tools within ZBrush designed for creating simplified armatures to guide complex sculpting processes. Their strength lies in their ability to simulate traditional sculptural armatures digitally, providing artists a robust method for laying out anatomy, proportions, and pose before sculpting detail.

Creating ZSphere Armatures

ZSpheres begin as a single, central sphere. Additional spheres are connected by drawing out from the center sphere, forming limbs, branches, or appendages, much like shaping a traditional wire armature.

To build a ZSphere skeleton for anatomical reference:

1. Select the ZSphere tool from the Tool palette.

2. Activate symmetry as needed to maintain anatomical accuracy. Symmetrical armatures simplify human or creature design.

3. Add spheres sequentially to form key joints and anatomical landmarks—shoulders, elbows, hips, knees, wrists, and ankles. Placing ZSpheres strategically defines basic anatomy clearly and quickly.

4. Adjust spheres using Move, Scale, and Rotate functions. Move spheres into proper alignment for accurate proportions, and scale spheres to indicate the relative mass of anatomical features.

For example, to construct a humanoid armature:

- Begin with the torso as the primary sphere.

- Extend spheres upwards for the neck and head.

- Draw spheres horizontally for shoulders, downwards for arms, and continue similarly for legs and feet.

Anatomical Accuracy and Proportions

ZSpheres allow easy visual adjustments to proportions:

- Accurate anatomy relies heavily on proportional relationships. Establish basic landmarks early to simplify accurate measurement.

- ZSphere positioning directly influences later sculpting stages, as the underlying armature dictates surface flow, muscle placement, and joint articulation.

- Frequent reference to anatomical images or anatomical charts during ZSphere armature creation ensures realistic outcomes.

Establish proportional guidelines using classical human proportion systems, such as the eight-head rule, to maintain structural integrity throughout the modeling process.

Using ZSpheres for Complex Creature Armatures

ZSpheres excel beyond humanoid anatomy. Their flexible nature allows artists to construct armatures for fantastical creatures, multi-limbed organisms, or intricate animal anatomy:

- Create multiple branching limb structures to represent wings, tails, tentacles, or additional appendages.

- Use varied sphere sizing to reflect muscle and bone structure diversity in non-human anatomy.

For creature designs, ZSphere armatures enable experimentation with balance, posture, and feasibility of unconventional anatomy before extensive sculpting begins.

Sculpting Directly with ZSketch Volume Brushes

After establishing a solid ZSphere armature, ZSketch provides a unique sculpting method that resembles adding clay to a physical armature. Instead of directly manipulating polygonal surfaces, ZSketch artists build form with brush strokes that add volume onto the ZSphere structure. This process mimics traditional additive clay sculpture, promoting intuitive and organic form-building.

Activating and Configuring ZSketch

To begin ZSketch sculpting:

1. With the ZSphere armature active, enable Edit mode.

2. Navigate to the ZSketch panel within the Tool palette, and activate Edit Sketch mode.

3. A unique set of ZSketch brushes become available, specifically designed to add, remove, or refine ZSketch volume.

Configurable settings in ZSketch brushes include stroke size, strength, and smoothness. These parameters control volume buildup precisely, ensuring optimal control during sculpting.

Volume Building with ZSketch Brushes

ZSketch strokes apply volume directly onto armatures:

- **Sketch1 and Sketch2 brushes**: Ideal for establishing initial mass and primary muscle groups. Rapid, controlled strokes deposit substantial volume quickly.

- **Smooth Brush**: Essential for refining transitions between added volumes, gently blending forms, and creating natural anatomical structures.

- **Bulge Brush**: Adds rounded, organic volume ideal for muscle masses, fleshy protrusions, or anatomical bulges.

- **Flush Brush**: Removes excess volume gently, reshaping existing strokes and maintaining controlled volumes.

When sculpting muscles or fleshy forms, apply strokes directionally along anatomical muscle fibers to produce realistic volume flow and tension patterns.

Layered ZSketch Techniques for Anatomical Precision

ZSketch sculpting benefits greatly from a layered approach:

- Begin with primary masses, sketching broad muscle groups and torso shapes.

- Gradually layer secondary anatomical features, refining muscle insertions, joint articulations, and connective tissues.

- Finish with tertiary details such as skin folds, minor muscle separations, or bony protrusions.

Artists typically build major muscle groups first—pectorals, deltoids, biceps, and quadriceps—followed by secondary forms such as tendons, connective tissues, and finer anatomical details. Layered volume application provides consistent anatomical realism, clearly defining each structural element.

Converting ZSketch into Base Meshes

Once satisfactory volumes are established using ZSketch, converting these sketches into polygonal base meshes facilitates detailed sculpting, retopology, or further refinement. This transition is critical for integrating ZSketch creations into standard sculpting and modeling workflows.

Generating Unified Skin from ZSketch

ZBrush converts ZSketch forms into polygonal geometry through the Unified Skin function:

1. In the Tool palette, access the Unified Skin submenu.

2. Adjust parameters such as Resolution, Density, and Smoothness. Higher resolution captures detailed forms accurately, whereas lower resolution generates simplified, topology-friendly geometry.

3. Click "Make Unified Skin" to generate polygonal mesh from ZSketch volumes.

Unified Skin meshes typically have dense, evenly-distributed polygon counts ideal for high-resolution sculpting but may require retopology for animation or production-ready purposes.

Adaptive Skin for Animation-Ready Meshes

Alternatively, Adaptive Skin generates geometry closely aligned with underlying ZSphere armatures, offering topology beneficial for animation or posing:

- Enable Adaptive Skin within the ZSphere subtool.

- Adjust Density to control subdivision levels; higher density increases polygonal detail, while lower density yields more efficient, simpler topology.

- Click "Make Adaptive Skin" to convert the ZSphere and ZSketch combined volumes into a clean, animation-friendly mesh.

Adaptive Skin maintains topology flow conducive to deformation, ideal for characters intended for posing or animation purposes.

Dynamic Posing with Adaptive Skin

Adaptive Skin meshes derived from ZSphere armatures retain direct connections to original armatures, facilitating dynamic posing early in the sculpting process. This capability provides sculptors with significant advantages, allowing them to test anatomical proportions, character poses, and balance intuitively without extensive rigging or deformation techniques.

Posing Adaptive Skin Meshes

To pose Adaptive Skin meshes dynamically:

- With the Adaptive Skin mesh selected, enter Transpose mode by pressing Move, Scale, or Rotate.

- Activate symmetry if appropriate, to mirror limb or anatomical adjustments efficiently.

- Select individual joints (ZSpheres) and apply transformations using the Transpose tool's handles. Adjust poses interactively in real-time.

- Preview adaptive skin results after posing adjustments by toggling preview mode, ensuring accurate surface deformation and anatomical correctness.

Adaptive Skin posing allows rapid iteration and exploration of character stances, gestures, and actions, helping artists visualize character attitude and anatomical realism from the earliest sculpting stages.

Maintaining Anatomical Integrity During Posing

Posing adaptive skin meshes requires attention to anatomical principles:

- Rotate joints within realistic physiological ranges to prevent unnatural stretching or compression of geometry.

- Regularly switch between adaptive skin preview and ZSphere skeleton views to verify anatomical accuracy.

- If pose adjustments cause distortion, revert to ZSphere or ZSketch volumes for corrective refinement before finalizing the adaptive skin mesh.

Dynamic posing thus serves both creative exploration and anatomical validation roles, improving sculptural outcomes by highlighting potential issues early, saving considerable correction time during subsequent detailed sculpting or rigging stages.

Iterative Posing for Concept Development

Adaptive skin posing greatly enhances conceptual exploration for character and creature designs:

- Experiment with multiple pose variations rapidly to explore character personality or action sequences.

- Use adaptive posing as reference for narrative-driven designs, storytelling-driven sculptures, or sequential character presentation.

- Iterate between ZSketch refinement and adaptive posing to progressively develop highly detailed, anatomically believable characters ready for high-end detailing.

This dynamic workflow seamlessly integrates structural modeling, anatomical refinement, and expressive posing, significantly enhancing creative flexibility, anatomical accuracy, and overall artistic efficiency.

Artists mastering ZSketch and advanced ZSphere armature techniques gain powerful methods for intuitive, organic modeling, anatomical accuracy, and expressive posing, firmly establishing these workflows as critical components of professional digital sculpting processes.

Scripting and Automation with ZScript

The digital sculpting process in ZBrush can involve many repetitive tasks—tasks that consume valuable time and energy, often distracting artists from their creative workflow. ZScript, ZBrush's built-in scripting language, provides a powerful and efficient method for automating these repetitive actions, enhancing productivity, and customizing the sculpting environment. By mastering ZScript, artists can significantly streamline their workflow, freeing more time for creative exploration and refinement of their work.

This chapter thoroughly explores the fundamentals of ZScript, including its interface, core scripting logic, automating repetitive sculpting tasks, developing custom tool macros, and creating intuitive buttons and panels to optimize usability and accessibility.

Introduction to ZScript Interface and Logic

ZScript is ZBrush's native scripting environment, allowing users to create customized automation routines directly within the software. The language is specifically tailored for ZBrush functionality, providing intuitive yet extensive control over sculpting, painting, and model management tasks.

Understanding the ZScript Environment

ZScript files have the `.zsc` extension, and scripts are typically stored in the ZBrush directory within a dedicated "ZScripts" folder. Each script can contain commands that control various elements of the ZBrush interface, allowing precise actions like toggling visibility, manipulating geometry, applying textures, or adjusting interface layouts.

To create or run a script:

1. Open the ZScript palette within ZBrush.

2. Load a ZScript file through the "Load" command.

3. Execute the script, observing ZBrush automatically perform the scripted actions.

Scripts can also run silently, meaning they execute without visual feedback, optimizing processing time and resource management.

Basic ZScript Logic and Syntax

ZScript uses straightforward syntax, consisting of clearly defined commands enclosed in square brackets. Each command includes parameters or modifiers specifying exactly what actions to perform and under what conditions.

For example, a basic script command to select a brush might look like:

[IPress,Brush:Standard]

Here, IPress instructs ZBrush to simulate pressing a button or tool within the interface. Brush:Standard references the specific tool or button.

ZScript also includes conditional logic for advanced functionality, using commands like [If], [Else], [Loop], and [RoutineCall]:

```
[If,[IExists,Tool:PolyMesh3D],
    [IPress,Tool:PolyMesh3D],
    [Note,"PolyMesh3D not found."]
]
```

This snippet checks if the PolyMesh3D tool exists and selects it; otherwise, it displays an error notification. Such logic allows scripts to adapt to varying interface states and conditions dynamically.

Variables and Data Management

ZScript supports variables, enabling the storage and manipulation of data within scripts. Variables can store numeric or text values, facilitating calculations, conditional operations, and dynamic adjustments to script behavior.

For instance:

[VarDef,size,50]
[ISet,Draw:Draw Size,#size]

This script defines a variable size set to 50 and then applies this value to ZBrush's Draw Size slider. Variables simplify script adjustments by centralizing values, allowing easy tweaking and fine-tuning.

Automating Repetitive Actions

One of ZScript's primary strengths lies in automating repetitive tasks. Actions frequently repeated during sculpting—such as subdividing meshes, exporting assets, setting up render passes, or preparing files for external software—can be automated, significantly reducing production time.

Recording Actions as ZScripts

ZBrush conveniently allows users to record their actions directly as ZScripts. This feature captures every interaction within the software interface, translating user operations into script commands.

To record actions:

1. Open the ZScript palette and select "Record."

2. Perform the desired tasks within ZBrush (e.g., subdivide a model, apply materials).

3. End recording via the "End Record" command.

4. Save the generated script file, now containing all recorded actions.

Recorded scripts provide immediate workflow enhancement without extensive scripting knowledge. Artists can refine recorded scripts by editing commands directly, optimizing sequences for efficiency and clarity.

Batch Processing with Scripts

Automation is especially beneficial for batch processing multiple assets, such as exporting numerous subtools simultaneously or uniformly applying texture or UV setups across multiple models.

Consider a simple script for batch exporting multiple subtools:

```
[Loop,[SubToolGetCount],
  [SubToolSelect,[Val,n]]
  [FileNameSetNext,[StrMerge,"Exported_",[SubToolGetName,[Val,n]],".obj"]]
  [IPress,Tool:Export]
,n]
```

This script cycles through each subtool, automatically exporting it with a structured naming convention. Automation of this nature drastically improves efficiency when working with large numbers of assets or models requiring identical treatment.

Automating Scene Setup

ZScript is invaluable in automating common scene setup procedures. For instance, applying standard render settings, turning on floor grids, or activating symmetry can all be scripted:

```
[IPress,Transform:Activate Symmetry]
[ISet,Render:BPR Shadows:Strength,0.75]
[IPress,Draw:Floor]
```

Running this simple script instantly configures the scene for consistent starting conditions, streamlining the setup process each time a new sculpting session begins.

Creating Custom Tool Macros

Macros are simplified ZScripts that run specific tasks or series of actions with a single button press. Macros significantly enhance workflow efficiency by allowing rapid execution of frequently repeated, routine operations without requiring deep scripting knowledge each time.

Creating Basic Macros

To create a macro in ZBrush:

1. Open the Macro menu and select "New Macro."

2. Perform the desired action or series of actions (e.g., subdivide mesh three times).

3. Return to the Macro menu and click "End Macro." Save and name your macro appropriately.

Macros appear directly in the Macro palette and can be triggered by clicking or assigning hotkeys. Typical macros might involve setting standard brush sizes, toggling visibility of multiple subtools simultaneously, or quickly applying favorite materials.

Editing and Customizing Macros

Recorded macros can be edited by directly modifying their underlying ZScript code. For example, a macro recorded to subdivide geometry can be edited to adjust subdivision levels or include error checking:

[If,[IExists,Tool:Geometry:Divide],

```
[Loop,3,
    [IPress,Tool:Geometry:Divide]
]
,
    [Note,"Divide function unavailable."]
]
```

Such customization ensures macros remain robust, flexible, and responsive to changing scenarios within the ZBrush environment.

Building User-Friendly Buttons and Panels

Beyond automation, ZScript enables artists to design customized interface elements—such as buttons, sliders, and comprehensive control panels—that directly integrate within ZBrush's standard interface. Creating custom UI components significantly improves accessibility, allowing quick access to regularly used scripts and tools.

Creating Custom Buttons

Custom buttons streamline the ZBrush workspace, offering one-click access to scripts or macros. Buttons can be defined clearly within a ZScript file using the [IButton] command:

```
[IButton,"My Tools:Quick Export","Exports active subtool.",
    [FileNameSetNext,"QuickExport.obj"]
    [IPress,Tool:Export]
]
```

This script creates a new button labeled "Quick Export" that appears under the custom palette named "My Tools." Clicking this button immediately exports the current subtool as "QuickExport.obj," simplifying frequent exports.

Building Custom UI Panels

More complex custom UI elements, such as full panels with grouped buttons and sliders, further enhance usability and organization. Panels are created with [ISubPalette] and populated with custom buttons and controls:

[ISubPalette,"My Tools:Quick Adjustments"]

```
[IButton,"My Tools:Quick Adjustments:Set High Res","Sets subdivision to 5",
  [Loop,5,
    [IPress,Tool:Geometry:Divide]
  ]
]
```

```
[IButton,"My Tools:Quick Adjustments:Symmetry On","Activates symmetry",
  [IPress,Transform:Activate Symmetry]
]
```

```
[ISlider,"My Tools:Quick Adjustments:Brush Size",50,1,1,100,"Adjusts brush size",
  [ISet,Draw:Draw Size,[IGet,"My Tools:Quick Adjustments:Brush Size"]]
]
```

This script defines a panel named "Quick Adjustments" containing multiple interactive controls. Users can easily set mesh subdivision, toggle symmetry, and quickly adjust brush sizes without navigating multiple interface menus, significantly enhancing workflow efficiency.

Customizing Interface Placement and Hotkeys

Once scripts and panels are created, artists can further optimize their ZBrush workspace by assigning custom interface elements to convenient locations and binding them to hotkeys:

- Drag custom buttons and panels directly onto the workspace for quick access.

- Assign hotkeys to custom buttons via ZBrush's Preferences menu, further accelerating workflow.

These personalized enhancements reduce navigation complexity and boost sculpting productivity, allowing artists to stay immersed in their creative processes without unnecessary interruptions.

By mastering ZScript fundamentals, automating repetitive actions, developing tailored macros, and integrating user-friendly interface elements, artists transform ZBrush into a personalized, powerful sculpting platform tailored precisely to their workflow needs. The effective use of scripting automation significantly streamlines creative processes, fostering greater efficiency and artistic freedom.

Rendering with External Shaders and PBR Workflows

Rendering a digital sculpture accurately in external rendering engines involves more than just exporting geometry. Artists aiming for photorealistic or visually coherent results must carefully manage texture maps, shader setups, and adhere strictly to physically based rendering (PBR) standards. Using external renderers such as Blender's Cycles, Arnold, or Redshift significantly extends creative possibilities, allowing more sophisticated lighting, realistic materials, and highly detailed final outputs compared to internal rendering methods. This chapter comprehensively covers the essential processes involved: exporting necessary maps from ZBrush, understanding physically based material concepts, constructing consistent shaders suitable for production, and ensuring PBR textures translate accurately between popular rendering engines.

Exporting Maps for External Renderers (Cycles, Arnold, Redshift)

The first step towards integrating ZBrush sculpted assets into external render pipelines involves careful extraction and exporting of texture maps. These maps include displacement, normal, roughness, metallic, ambient occlusion (AO), and diffuse (albedo) textures, each critical for producing accurate and visually compelling results.

Displacement and Normal Map Exporting

Displacement and normal maps convey surface detail effectively without requiring heavy geometry. ZBrush's Multi Map Exporter tool simplifies exporting these maps specifically tailored for external renderers.

- **Displacement Maps**:

    - Go to **ZPlugin > Multi Map Exporter**.

- ○ Select "Displacement" and set export settings to 32-bit EXR for maximum fidelity.

- ○ Ensure "Flip V" is enabled, as ZBrush's vertical UV coordinates differ from most external render engines.

- **Normal Maps**:

  - ○ Use the same Multi Map Exporter interface.

  - ○ Export as tangent-space normal maps in 16-bit PNG or TIFF formats.

  - ○ Also flip vertically to match external UV coordinate standards.

These maps should precisely match the exported base geometry to avoid mismatches or render artifacts. Always verify UV integrity prior to exporting maps.

Albedo and Roughness Maps

Albedo maps capture color without lighting information. To export albedo:

- Ensure the model has accurate Polypaint data applied.

- Export the Polypaint as textures directly via the Texture Map palette or Multi Map Exporter.

- Save as high-quality PNG or TIFF formats.

Roughness maps control reflectivity, indicating surface smoothness. While ZBrush doesn't generate roughness directly, artists typically create them externally (e.g., Substance Painter or Photoshop). However, ZBrush-generated

AO or cavity maps can serve as useful masks or starting points for roughness texture development.

Exporting Metallic and Ambient Occlusion Maps

Metallic maps indicate which parts of a surface are metallic versus dielectric:

- Generally created externally, metallic maps define metals as pure white and non-metals black.

- ZBrush's polypainting capabilities facilitate basic metallic masking if planned carefully.

Ambient Occlusion maps:

- Generated within ZBrush using Masking tools or Multi Map Exporter AO baking.

- Useful in external shading for adding depth and subtle shading variation, particularly in recessed areas.

Each of these maps, carefully exported and checked, ensures accurate rendering results in external applications.

Introduction to Physically Based Material Standards

Physically based rendering (PBR) standards define consistent rules for material creation across different software. By adhering strictly to these rules, artists achieve predictable, realistic results regardless of renderer choice.

Understanding PBR Principles

PBR relies on scientifically derived rules dictating how light interacts with surfaces. Fundamental principles include energy conservation, meaning surfaces never reflect more light than they receive, and microfacet theory, which describes roughness and reflectivity at microscopic levels. Materials under PBR must follow real-world reflectance values, drastically improving realism.

Two principal PBR workflows exist:

- **Metalness/Roughness Workflow**:

    - Commonly used in real-time engines like Unity and Unreal Engine, as well as renderers like Blender Cycles and Redshift.

    - Requires metallic, roughness, albedo, and normal maps.

- **Specular/Glossiness Workflow**:

    - Often associated with older rendering systems, still widely used in film pipelines.

    - Employs specular and glossiness maps instead of metallic and roughness.

Modern workflows predominantly use the Metalness/Roughness approach due to its simplicity and realism.

Defining Realistic Values

Real-world materials have specific reflectivity (albedo) ranges:

- Metals typically exhibit high reflectivity, darker albedo, and colored specular reflections (e.g., gold, copper).

- Non-metals (dielectrics) feature higher albedo values, low reflectivity, and grayscale specular reflections.

Accurately referencing real-world values from material databases helps artists ensure materials behave realistically across lighting conditions.

Building Consistent Shaders for Production

Consistency is crucial in professional rendering pipelines. Developing robust, reusable shader networks ensures predictable outputs, rapid material iteration, and reduces setup time dramatically.

Creating Shader Networks in Blender Cycles

Cycles nodes typically require albedo, normal, roughness, and metallic textures:

- Start with a Principled BSDF shader node.

- Connect the exported albedo texture to the "Base Color" input.

- Attach roughness and metallic maps directly into their respective inputs.

- Connect normal maps through a Normal Map node before plugging into the normal input.

For displacement details, utilize a Displacement node combined with displacement maps. Set displacement to "displacement and bump" mode in the Cycles render settings to ensure proper high-frequency surface detail representation.

Shader Setups in Arnold

Arnold employs the aiStandardSurface shader, aligning closely with the Principled BSDF approach:

- Albedo textures plug into the "Base Color."

- Metallic maps go into the "Metalness" attribute.

- Roughness maps connect directly to "Specular Roughness."

- Normal maps feed through an Arnold Normal Map node.

Arnold's displacement workflow requires connecting displacement maps to a separate shading engine or shape node's displacement slot, adjusting height accordingly to control depth and accuracy.

Shader Development in Redshift

Redshift's shader workflow is similarly straightforward:

- Utilize Redshift Material nodes, connecting albedo to the diffuse slot.

- Roughness maps connect to reflection roughness inputs.

- Metalness maps define metal attributes directly.

- Normals pass through Redshift's Bump Map node configured for tangent space normals.

Redshift handles displacement via the dedicated Redshift Displacement node, adjusting scale settings to match the intended displacement height.

Linking PBR Maps Across Rendering Engines

To achieve consistent appearances when transferring between renderers, accurately mapping PBR textures is vital. Subtle differences in interpretation may exist between software packages, so understanding these nuances ensures visual fidelity.

Ensuring Accurate UVs and Normals

Consistent results depend heavily on matching UV coordinates and normal map tangent spaces:

- Always verify UV orientations, flipping maps vertically if necessary, matching standards between ZBrush exports and renderer inputs.

- Confirm tangent space normal map conventions align; Cycles, Arnold, and Redshift typically adhere to the OpenGL normal map format.

Matching Roughness and Metalness Interpretation

Renderers interpret roughness slightly differently:

- Blender Cycles expects roughness maps linearly interpreted from 0 (smooth) to 1 (fully rough).

- Arnold similarly uses a linear roughness interpretation, requiring little adjustment from standard textures.

- Redshift can require slight adjustments to roughness levels, ensuring visual consistency matches intended realism across materials.

Metalness maps generally translate seamlessly across renderers. However, checking documentation or renderer-specific guidelines can help confirm precise implementation.

Color Space Management and Linear Workflow

A critical aspect often overlooked is color space consistency:

- All render engines typically expect linear-space textures except for albedo, which uses sRGB.

- Set roughness, metallic, AO, and displacement maps explicitly to linear space in external renderers.

- Albedo maps should remain in sRGB or gamma-corrected space for accurate color reproduction.

Strict adherence to linear workflow standards across renderers ensures consistent visual fidelity.

Cross-Renderer Consistency Checks

Always perform quick tests when transferring materials between renderers:

- Render identical scenes or test assets using minimal lighting setups in each renderer.

- Compare results side-by-side, adjusting roughness or displacement scales minimally to match visual outputs.

- Document any adjustments clearly, ensuring repeatability and workflow consistency across future projects.

This methodical approach guarantees shaders and materials maintain uniformity, essential for professional pipeline integrity and visual coherence across different rendering software.

Through carefully exporting maps, understanding PBR standards, meticulously crafting shaders, and managing consistent translation of textures, artists ensure seamless integration of ZBrush-sculpted assets into external rendering environments. Adopting these detailed, structured workflows dramatically enhances productivity and visual accuracy, essential qualities in modern digital production.

Sculpting for 3D Printing and Physical Output

3D printing has become an essential extension of digital sculpting, bridging virtual creation with physical realization. ZBrush, known for its sculpting capabilities, provides all the necessary tools to prepare high-resolution models for reliable 3D print output. This chapter outlines the best practices and advanced techniques for transforming digital sculpts into print-ready assets. Topics covered include preparing watertight meshes, correcting non-manifold geometry, hollowing and keying models for assembly, and properly exporting files for both resin and fused deposition modeling (FDM) printers.

Preparing Watertight Models

A watertight model, also referred to as a manifold mesh, is crucial for successful 3D printing. This means that the model must be a closed volume with no gaps, holes, or intersecting geometry. Printers interpret geometry as solid forms, and any open edges can confuse slicing software or cause failed prints.

Identifying Watertightness

ZBrush does not display open edges as clearly as some polygonal modeling software, but several tools assist in verifying model integrity:

- Use **Tool > Geometry > Mesh Integrity** to check for errors. Click "Check Mesh Integrity" to analyze whether the model has unconnected points or open edges.

- The **Polygroup** visualization can sometimes reveal problem areas when unexpected group splits appear in flat regions.

- Running **Tool > Geometry > Modify Topology > Close Holes** provides a quick solution for minor missing surface areas, although care must be taken as it may generate unexpected topology.

Best Practices for Watertight Sculpting

- Avoid overlapping subtools when possible. While visually effective in renders, overlapping meshes can confuse slicing software and produce unpredictable results in physical form.

- Use **Merge Down** to combine subtools, followed by **DynaMesh** to fuse overlapping parts into a continuous volume.

- Keep resolution consistent across all merged parts to avoid mesh artifacts and ensure a seamless union during Dynamesh operations.

- After DynaMeshing, always reproject detail from the original sculpt using **SubTool > Project All**, ensuring no detail is lost during the conversion.

Fixing Non-Manifold Geometry

Non-manifold geometry includes floating vertices, internal faces, zero-thickness walls, or edges that share more than two faces. These issues can severely disrupt the slicing process and result in errors during printing.

Detecting Non-Manifold Geometry

While ZBrush does not highlight non-manifold issues by default, certain workflows expose them:

- Use **Decimation Master** to prepare your model for export. It will often fail or produce warnings if the model contains problematic geometry.

- Exporting your model into Netfabb Basic, Meshmixer, or Blender provides more detailed mesh diagnostics.

Corrective Techniques in ZBrush

- **Remesh By Union (ZRemesher)**: Found in the SubTool menu under Boolean operations, this function merges intersecting meshes and removes overlapping surfaces, generating clean topology suitable for printing.

- **DynaMesh with Polish Enabled**: This can eliminate internal faces and smooth surface transitions, especially when resolution is carefully managed.

- **ZRemesher with Guide Curves**: After cleaning with DynaMesh, ZRemesher can produce quad-based topology more suitable for slicing and for use in engineering software downstream.

Edge Inspection

Even if the model appears clean, it's important to zoom into junctions and surface intersections. If brushes or components were used to create sharp insets or overlapping seams, they may need additional mesh cleanup or be re-sculpted to fuse properly.

Hollowing, Keying, and Slicing Parts

Large models require optimization to print efficiently, both in terms of material consumption and build volume limitations. Hollowing and slicing are essential in this regard, and keying facilitates accurate reassembly post-printing.

Hollowing Models for Resin Printing

Hollowing reduces resin usage, print time, and internal pressure build-up during curing. In ZBrush, hollowing is performed using **Live Boolean** or **DynaMesh Subtraction**.

Steps for hollowing:

1. Duplicate your model and reduce its scale slightly using **Tool > Deformation > Size**.

2. Subtract the inner mesh from the outer using **Live Boolean** setup:

   ○ Set the inner mesh's subtool to subtractive mode.

   ○ Merge and **Make Boolean Mesh** to generate the hollowed version.

3. Alternatively, use **DynaMesh** with the inner mesh marked as subtractive.

Ensure a wall thickness of at least 1.5–2mm to retain strength while saving material. For large hollow objects, include **drainage holes** near the base using simple cylinder subtools set to subtractive mode, then reapply Boolean or DynaMesh operations.

Keying Parts for Assembly

Large models often exceed a printer's build volume or require segmentation for ease of painting and shipping. To maintain alignment and structural integrity during assembly, keys are used to physically align and attach parts.

Techniques:

- Use **Insert Mesh Brushes** (IMM) to add pre-designed peg shapes.

- Create custom keys with primitive cubes or cylinders using subtractive Boolean operations.

- Design **male-female peg systems**, ensuring a tight fit. Test peg size tolerance depending on your printer's dimensional accuracy.

Always orient keys to assist gravity and assembly. Cylindrical pegs and square sockets prevent rotation, while rectangular keys prevent incorrect orientation during reassembly.

Slicing Models for FDM and Resin

For printers with build volume limitations, slicing must be done intelligently:

- Slice models in flat planes to minimize visible seams and maximize bed adhesion.

- Use **Live Boolean with cutting tools** (e.g., plane meshes) to segment the model. Remember to apply Boolean operations and remesh to resolve any new edges.

- Save each segment as an individual subtool or export separately for simplified printing.

Slicing tools outside ZBrush (e.g., Netfabb or Meshmixer) can also be used when fine-tuned control over seams and connections is required, especially in engineering contexts.

Exporting for Resin and FDM Printers (STL/OBJ Best Practices)

Once the sculpt is finalized and properly prepared, it must be exported in a format compatible with slicer software and printers. STL and OBJ are the primary file types used in 3D printing workflows.

Choosing the Right Format

- **STL**:

  - Most commonly used for both resin and FDM printers.

  - Stores mesh data as triangulated surfaces.

  - No support for color or material attributes.

- Use for simple, monochrome prints or when universal compatibility is required.

- **OBJ**:

  - Supports vertex color (polypaint), UV mapping, and multiple material zones.

  - Useful when printing full-color models or preparing files for multi-material printers.

Best Practices for Exporting

1. **Clean the mesh**:

   - Use **ZPlugin > 3D Print Hub** for mesh scaling and export.

   - Run **Unify Scale** only if working in default units; otherwise, apply correct real-world dimensions beforehand.

2. **Check normals**:

   - Recalculate or verify face normals to ensure the model faces outward. Inward-facing normals can result in invisible or incorrectly printed parts.

3. **Set proper resolution**:

   - Decimate the mesh using **Decimation Master** if file size becomes an issue.

   - Ensure enough resolution is preserved to maintain fine sculpted details.

4. **Export scale units**:

   o ZBrush exports in generic units, so confirm scale compatibility with your slicer. The 3D Print Hub plugin can convert dimensions to millimeters or inches as needed.

5. **Split large files**:

   o If your STL or OBJ exceeds practical limits (generally 500MB+), split the model into components before export.

   o Name exported files clearly with segment identifiers and scale references (e.g., "Torso_Upper_L.stl").

Resin-Specific Considerations

For resin printers:

- Prefer hollowed models with **drainage holes**, unless printing solid miniatures or jewelry.

- Ensure no closed voids exist internally; trapped resin can cure unpredictably.

- Export with watertight verification performed using third-party tools such as Meshmixer or Lychee Slicer validation tools.

FDM-Specific Considerations

For FDM printers:

- Orient parts flat to reduce warping.

- Add custom support towers only when needed—most slicers generate support automatically, but complex overhangs may benefit from manually sculpted supports.

- Use wider keys and consider tolerances for material shrinkage, especially when printing with ABS or PETG.

Adhering to these standards ensures that the final exported models maintain structural integrity, visual quality, and compatibility across various 3D printing technologies. Whether preparing intricate collectibles, mechanical prototypes, or artistic installations, precise mesh preparation and export discipline remain the foundation of successful physical realization of digital sculpture.

Non-Human Anatomy: Sculpting Creatures, Insects, and Fantasy Forms

Digital sculptors frequently move beyond traditional human forms to explore imaginative and complex subjects such as alien creatures, insectoid entities, and mythological hybrids. Although such designs depart from real-world anatomical norms, they still rely heavily on a sculptor's understanding of structure, proportion, and form consistency. Successful creature design stems from a disciplined application of anatomy fundamentals combined with creative extrapolation. This chapter explores key concepts and techniques for sculpting convincing non-human anatomy, constructing hybrid musculature, addressing unusual limb configurations, and balancing scale and symmetry in fantasy and science fiction contexts.

Anatomy References Outside Human Proportions

A common misconception in creature design is that anatomy becomes irrelevant when creating fictional beings. In truth, even the most unusual characters benefit from a clear underlying anatomical structure. This provides internal logic, stability in form, and visual believability.

Studying Comparative Anatomy

Real-world anatomy references are indispensable when designing non-human forms. Comparative anatomy—the study of similarities and differences in the anatomical structures of different species—offers a solid foundation for building unfamiliar designs.

Key reference categories:

- **Mammals**: Quadrupeds, marine mammals, and primates offer insight into variations in limb proportion and torso structure. Big cats and apes, for example, provide robust limb musculature and flexible spinal columns.

- **Birds and Bats**: Wing structures, talons, and digit manipulation patterns from avian and chiropteran anatomy serve as a basis for designing flying creatures.

- **Reptiles and Amphibians**: Tail articulation, elongated digits, and muscular crawling limbs offer a template for ground-based or climbing species.

- **Insects and Arachnids**: Carapace segmentation, exoskeletal joints, and eye placement provide structure for more alien, multi-limbed entities.

Cross-referencing skeletal and muscular systems from these categories allows sculptors to construct biologically plausible creatures while extending creative latitude.

Deviating from Human Scale and Proportion

When stepping outside human anatomy, proportional balance remains critical. Exaggerated limb lengths, heads, or torsos must still appear functional within the creature's environment.

Guidelines include:

- Ensure that limbs—no matter how stylized—visually support weight distribution.

- Oversized or undersized parts (e.g., claws, heads, tails) should be balanced by complementary anatomy such as reinforced joints or muscle groups.

- Use proportion as a storytelling tool—slender limbs might suggest speed, while massive forearms could imply strength or aggression.

This approach anchors exaggerated proportions in purpose, making even the most unusual designs feel coherent.

Designing Believable Alien or Insectoid Anatomy

Sculpting alien or insect-like creatures presents unique challenges due to the radical differences from vertebrate forms. Nonetheless, successful designs rely on consistent internal rules and surface cohesion.

Building an Insectoid Framework

Insect-based creatures differ from vertebrates in that their anatomy is defined by an exoskeleton rather than an internal skeletal and muscular system. This leads to visible segmentation and articulation along exterior forms.

Key characteristics:

- **Segmented Limbs**: Insect limbs typically consist of three to five segments: coxa, femur, tibia, tarsus, and claw. Mimicking these proportions preserves believability even when stylized.

- **Exoskeletal Plates**: Use overlapping forms to represent armor or body plates. Creases between plates should follow realistic joint directions for bending and rotation.

- **Bilateral Symmetry with Repetition**: Many arthropods exhibit mirrored limbs and repeated body structures. This repetition can be exploited to create rhythm in design but should be varied slightly to avoid monotony.

When creating humanoid-insect hybrids, blend these principles with vertebrate musculature to add volume and organic curvature beneath or between plates.

Alien Logic and Evolutionary Plausibility

Even abstract alien forms should be based on plausible biomechanical rules. Ask key design questions:

- How does the creature move? Are joints arranged logically for motion?

- Where is the creature's center of mass? Can it walk or stand without collapsing?

- How does the creature sense its environment? Where are its eyes, antennae, or equivalent sensory structures?

- How does the creature process energy? Consider mouth placement, respiratory structures, or digestive apertures.

Anchoring design decisions in speculative biology prevents the creature from becoming abstract noise and lends credibility to even the most surreal sculpt.

Surface Details and Skin Variation

Surface characteristics such as chitinous armor, slimy membranes, or spongy tissue give life to creature forms. Varying materials across the model—smooth vs. textured, soft vs. hard—adds richness and hierarchy.

Common sculpting tools for such surfaces include:

- **Orb Cracks and DamStandard**: For engraved lines and structural creases.

- **Surface Noise**: For granular skin detail or scale patterns.

- **Custom Alphas**: To create unique skin textures or repeating details across exoskeletal panels.

These tools allow sculptors to replicate biological texture diversity observed in real-world organisms.

Integrating Human Muscle Flow into Hybrid Forms

Blending human musculature with animalistic or alien designs is a common challenge in character design. The key is to maintain the natural flow of human anatomy while adapting it to altered proportions or limb structures.

Understanding Human Muscle Grouping

Before integrating human anatomy into a hybrid, sculptors must internalize core muscle systems:

- **Torso**: Includes pectorals, abdominals, latissimus dorsi, and trapezius.

- **Upper Limbs**: Biceps, triceps, deltoids, and forearm groups.

- **Lower Limbs**: Quadriceps, hamstrings, glutes, and calf muscles.

Each group flows naturally into adjacent forms, creating rhythm and cohesion in human anatomy. In hybrid creatures, this flow should be preserved even as limbs change orientation or proportion.

Adjusting Muscle Insertion and Origin

When limbs are modified—such as extended arms, backward-bending legs, or multi-jointed appendages—the origin and insertion of muscles must also be adjusted. Maintaining the logic of muscle function (i.e., contraction pulling from origin to insertion) helps build believable new forms.

Examples:

- A centaur-like creature would require the gluteal and spinal muscles to extend into a horse-like lower body.

- An aquatic humanoid may have broader latissimus dorsi to support stronger shoulder rotation for swimming.

- A four-armed hybrid might have duplicate deltoids and clavicles, layered or offset to maintain anatomical feasibility.

Use the human muscle map as a guide, but allow it to warp and adapt according to limb count and design objectives.

Sculpting Skin Flow and Tension

Even fantastical anatomy requires believable skin tension and fold patterns. Skin stretches across convex muscle bulges and compresses in joint folds. Capturing this dynamic is essential for conveying motion and weight.

Sculptors should:

- Build in overlapping muscle forms to simulate organic compression.

- Emphasize key landmarks such as collarbones, scapulae, and iliac crests—even in non-human designs—to ground anatomy.

- Use wrinkle brushes and smooth transitions between muscle groups to create natural deformation zones.

Even when forms are unfamiliar, realistic skin behavior reinforces believability.

Addressing Limb Count, Scale, and Symmetry Creatively

Creature design often requires adding or modifying limbs and altering the number of appendages. These changes, while stylistic, must still adhere to biological logic and visual balance.

Increasing Limb Count

Multiple limbs can suggest evolutionary adaptation, enhanced power, or otherworldly intelligence. To incorporate extra limbs:

- **Anchor them to believable bone structures**. For example, additional arms may emerge from a secondary shoulder girdle or modified ribcage.

- **Stagger joints** so that motion appears coordinated, not chaotic.

- **Offset the timing** of limb placement for gait logic, especially in crawling or climbing creatures.

Avoid simply duplicating human limbs without adjusting anatomical structures to support them.

Managing Limb Scale and Mass

Exaggerating limb size often conveys strength or agility, but scale must consider counterbalance and joint integrity:

- Heavily muscled limbs need robust joint articulation, particularly around hips and shoulders.

- Tiny limbs must have visible purpose, such as manipulation tools or sensory organs, or they risk appearing vestigial.

- Long limbs require strong spine and pelvis support, especially for bipedal stability.

Anchor oversized or undersized features in evolutionary purpose or biomechanical necessity.

Asymmetry and Functional Balance

Intentional asymmetry can suggest mutation, specialized evolution, or narrative uniqueness. However, asymmetry must retain structural coherence:

- Use asymmetry in surface detail, scarring, or equipment placement to suggest experience or culture.

- Allow major anatomical asymmetry only when balance is addressed—e.g., a large claw countered by a heavier tail or broader base.

- Mirror primary limbs and unbalance secondary ones to maintain silhouette integrity while adding visual interest.

Asymmetry is most effective when used sparingly and meaningfully, rather than arbitrarily.

Creating Unique Silhouettes

The overall silhouette determines first impressions. In non-human design, it must stand apart from familiar creatures while still communicating identity.

Effective silhouette practices:

- Prioritize distinct shapes at a distance—e.g., elongated tails, horn shapes, or limb orientation.

- Avoid over-detailing the silhouette; keep focal elements clean and bold.

- Design creature poses that reinforce gesture, even in static sculpture.

Non-human sculpting often starts with a silhouette sketch or primitive block-out before detail is added. The clearer the initial shape, the stronger the finished piece.

By building non-human anatomy on a framework of natural form logic, referencing real-world biology, adapting human structure intelligently, and applying balance in asymmetry and scale, sculptors produce original designs that feel authentic and visually compelling. These principles remain essential regardless of whether the subject is a mythological dragon, alien explorer, or biomechanical insectoid hybrid.

Advanced Use of Materials and MatCaps

Materials and MatCaps in ZBrush are more than visual overlays—they serve as essential sculpting aids, providing sculptors with vital feedback about surface curvature, microform, and detail flow. While basic users may rely on default settings, professional artists leverage custom MatCaps and real-time lighting materials to guide sculptural refinement, diagnose form issues, and craft polished presentations. This chapter explores the advanced methodologies for creating custom MatCaps, selecting and manipulating materials to enhance sculpting accuracy, configuring materials under purposeful lighting conditions, and exporting MatCap-like effects as texture maps for further use in rendering or real-time applications.

Creating Custom MatCaps for Sculpting and Presentation

MatCaps—short for Material Capture—are image-based materials that encode both surface shading and lighting in a single texture. Unlike dynamic shaders, MatCaps do not respond to light in real time but instead simulate lighting and material response using a baked-in reflection model. Because they reflect light from a fixed perspective, MatCaps are ideal for analyzing surface curvature and material fidelity during the sculpting process.

The Structure of a MatCap

Each MatCap includes a spherical image that encodes:

- Diffuse and specular light response.

- Reflectivity characteristics.

- Shadow falloff direction.

- Hue and saturation associated with material types (e.g., skin, clay, metal).

ZBrush uses this image to remap normals in real time, giving the illusion of depth and lighting interaction. This method works best when the sculpt is viewed from consistent angles, making it perfect for static evaluations, thumbnails, and promotional shots.

Creating a Custom MatCap

To create your own MatCap material:

1. **Render a sphere in an external program** with the lighting, shadows, and material look you want. This could be in KeyShot, Blender, Maya, or another renderer that supports global illumination and surface materials.

2. Export the rendered image at a square resolution—commonly 1024×1024 or higher. The light source should be aligned with the center of the sphere to maintain shading consistency.

3. In ZBrush, go to **Material > Create MatCap**, and import your custom image.

4. ZBrush applies the shading to all models using this MatCap. You can then refine the material attributes in the Material Modifiers palette.

MatCap Customization Options

Once imported, MatCaps can be modified to enhance usability:

- Adjust **specular intensity** and **diffuse levels** to emphasize or reduce material brightness.

- Modify **ambient** and **cavity settings** to control shadow depth perception.

- Experiment with **noise overlays** for materials like skin or concrete to simulate pore structure or granular surface textures.

MatCaps can also include sculpting-friendly enhancements like contrast overlays to boost form visibility at micro-detail levels. Save these variations under different names to switch between them as needed for sculpting versus presentation tasks.

Organizing and Saving Custom Libraries

To ensure MatCaps are reusable:

- Save them using **Material > Save As** into the ZBrush "ZStartup/Materials" directory.

- Restart ZBrush to load them automatically into your default session.

- For larger MatCap libraries, organize by category (skin, metal, stylized) and consider using prefixes (e.g., "SKN_RedClay.ZMT") to keep them easily sortable.

Proper organization supports a production-friendly workflow, especially when switching between design phases or team members.

Using Materials to Read Surface Quality During Sculpt

Advanced sculptors use different materials to reveal different aspects of form. Some materials are ideal for detecting volume issues, while others help analyze fine surface breakups such as pores, wrinkles, or micro-creases. Swapping materials regularly improves critical evaluation and leads to higher-quality surface results.

Identifying Form Using Clay-Style Materials

Clay-style materials—such as Red Wax, Mahogany, or custom gray clay MatCaps—are ideal for sculpting primary and secondary forms. Their mid-contrast shading and moderate specular properties highlight changes in plane direction and help evaluate large-volume transitions.

Use cases:

- **Volume confirmation**: Check transitions from ribcage to abdomen or thigh to knee.

- **Edge balance**: Verify that muscle insertions or character folds follow natural arcs.

- **Contour refinement**: Easily observe edge sharpness and silhouette consistency.

Diagnosing Surface Microdetails with Specular Materials

High-specular materials such as Basic Material 2 or custom glossy MatCaps simulate hard lighting, making it easier to detect unwanted surface noise, brush streaking, or unintentional planar shifts. They are essential during high-frequency sculpting phases.

Use cases:

- **Pore pattern detection**: Reveal uniformity or natural randomness of skin detail.

- **Stroke correction**: Identify when brush alphas are causing visible repetition.

- **Cavity smoothing**: Verify that valleys and ridges are behaving naturally under light.

Materials with fine noise baked into their texture can simulate surface tension, providing enhanced feedback when pushing or pulling form at tertiary levels.

Switching Materials Strategically

Integrate material changes into your evaluation routine:

- Use **hotkeys or custom interface buttons** to toggle between 2–3 primary materials.

- Assign purpose-based materials: one for volume, one for microdetail, one for presentation.

- Train your visual analysis by rotating your sculpt and observing how the material reveals its structure under different orientations.

Such habits help detect subtle issues early, minimizing time spent on post-sculpt cleanup or rework.

Lighting Materials for Sculpting Feedback

Even though MatCaps bake lighting into the material, ZBrush's dynamic materials respond to real light. For custom shaders, lighting plays a pivotal role in evaluating shape accuracy and spatial relationships.

Configuring Light Placement

ZBrush allows adjustment of up to eight lights. Most sculptors use a primary key light with fill and rim lights to simulate natural environmental lighting:

- Access **Light > Position Sphere** to drag the light source around the model.

- Adjust **Intensity, Shadow, and Ambient** sliders to find the ideal illumination for your material.

- For directional inspection, use a **rim light** placed opposite the camera to highlight edges and transitions.

This setup mimics three-point lighting, useful for both sculpt feedback and presentation renders.

Sculpting Under Dynamic Light Conditions

Use lighting adjustments in combination with materials to:

- Identify abrupt transitions in anatomical regions.

- Highlight symmetrical inconsistencies.

- Reveal undercut regions where shadows become dense or geometry occludes itself.

Dynamic lighting enables real-time evaluation from different visual angles, an advantage MatCaps do not provide. Toggle between MatCap and dynamic shaders as needed to evaluate form holistically.

Storing and Reusing Light Setups

To ensure lighting consistency:

- Save lighting rigs using the **Light > Save** function.

- Reload specific setups depending on whether you're sculpting, posing, or rendering.

- Consider saving light settings alongside material snapshots for exact visual recall during revisions.

This workflow maintains consistency across multiple sculpt sessions or among multiple team members in production environments.

Baking MatCap-Style Renders into Textures

MatCaps are frequently used not only during sculpting but also in final presentation or asset baking. In many workflows, especially in game development or stylized rendering pipelines, it's desirable to bake the MatCap effect directly into a texture.

Setting Up for Bake

Before baking:

1. Apply UVs to your model using **UV Master** or external unwrapping software.

2. Assign the chosen MatCap material.

3. Verify that polypaint is turned off, as it can override material preview.

Baking a MatCap to Texture

ZBrush offers a render-to-texture feature using its **BPR (Best Preview Render)** system and the **Texture > GrabDoc** workflow:

1. Align your model in the desired view (usually orthographic front, side, etc.).

2. Click **Render > BPR Render**.

3. Navigate to the **Document** palette and use **ZGrabber or GrabDoc** to capture the rendered image.

4. Export the result as a flattened image with embedded MatCap shading.

Alternatively, use **Render > BPR to Texture Map** plugins or scripts to automate baking into UV space if needed for stylized games or real-time presentation.

Considerations When Baking MatCaps

While MatCaps are fast and visually rich, they do not store physical lighting data. Use them for:

- **Stylized character sheets**.

- **Turntable renders**.

- **Static object displays**.

Avoid them in dynamic environments where lighting changes, such as real-time game engines, unless the baked result is used as a flat, unchanging display texture.

Export Formats and Presentation Uses

Once baked:

- Export as PNG or TIFF with transparency if using overlays.

- Combine with normal maps, cavity maps, and AO maps in compositing software to build layered renders.

- Use baked MatCaps for quick previews in art portfolios, turnarounds, or printed model sheets.

Professional workflows often incorporate baked MatCaps into quick client previews, saving rendering time while maintaining presentation quality.

Conclusion

The Evolution of Your Craft as a Digital Sculptor

As you reach the end of this comprehensive guide, it's important to reflect on how far you've come and where your journey as a digital sculptor is headed. The world of digital sculpting is a dynamic, ever-evolving field, constantly driven by technological innovations, creative exploration, and the growing demands of industries that rely on digital art. The tools and techniques you've learned are just the beginning, and as you continue to refine your skills, new opportunities will emerge, each more exciting and challenging than the last.

The Lifelong Nature of Mastery

One of the key takeaways from this journey is that mastery in digital sculpting, much like in any other artistic discipline, is not something that happens overnight. It requires dedication, consistent practice, and the willingness to push boundaries. You've gained access to a treasure trove of tools, methodologies, and strategies that will elevate your work. However, the real growth happens when you begin experimenting on your own, adapting what you've learned to suit your unique artistic vision.

The process of sculpting digitally isn't just about manipulating polygons or applying textures; it's about bringing an idea to life in a way that is both technically sound and artistically expressive. As you continue your work, don't be afraid to take risks and explore new directions. Innovation in this field doesn't come from following rules—it comes from breaking them.

Embracing Innovation and Change

The digital sculpting space is defined by constant innovation. With each update to software, new plugins, and evolving workflows, you are presented with opportunities to adapt and grow your craft. From the early days of digital modeling to the current advancements in artificial intelligence, procedural generation, and enhanced rendering techniques, the pace of change has been rapid. Keeping up with these developments is crucial, as they will not only influence the tools you use but also inspire fresh ways of thinking about your work.

By experimenting with the latest software features and integrating new techniques, you can push the limits of your creativity. Whether it's utilizing advanced brush settings or exploring cutting-edge AI integration, staying informed about emerging trends and incorporating them into your work will set you apart from others in the field.

Creating Work That Speaks for Itself

As you advance in your sculpting journey, the importance of building a strong portfolio cannot be overstated. Your portfolio is a reflection of your skills, creativity, and personal style. It is a tool that showcases not just what you can do, but how you think and approach problems. The work you create must tell a story—whether it's through the intricate details of a character model, the precision of a hard surface design, or the overall narrative of a piece.

Curating your portfolio is a process in itself. It's about selecting your best work, but also about showing a variety of skills. The diversity in your portfolio should not only reflect technical proficiency but also creativity, problem-solving, and the ability to work on a variety of projects across different styles and genres.

The digital world is highly visual, and with platforms like ArtStation, Behance, and personal websites, your work can reach an international audience. Don't hesitate to share your creative process through blogs, video tutorials, or social media, as these platforms allow you to build a professional network and engage with like-minded artists and potential clients. Building your online presence is as much a part of your sculpting career as the work itself.

Building a Sustainable Career

The path to becoming a successful digital sculptor extends beyond honing your technical skills. Building a career in this field requires an understanding of the industry, networking, and continuous learning. Whether you work as a freelancer, in-house artist, or in collaboration with other professionals, it's important to approach your career with a mindset that blends creativity with professionalism.

A career in digital sculpting can take many forms. You might specialize in game asset creation, character design for films, or 3D printing. You could even venture into teaching and mentoring the next generation of artists. The key is to find your niche and continuously evolve within it. Professionalism, in both your artistic work and your business practices, will distinguish you in the competitive digital art landscape.

Networking with other professionals, attending industry conferences (virtual or in-person), and taking part in collaborative projects are essential for staying connected. These interactions can lead to opportunities for career growth, whether through a new job, partnership, or a freelance project.

The Impact of Your Work

At its best, digital sculpting is more than a craft—it's an art form with the power to evoke emotion, tell stories, and spark new ideas. Your creations can become part of larger narratives in games, films, and other forms of media. Each digital model you create has the potential to leave an impact, shaping the visual storytelling of the projects it's part of.

As you continue to develop your skills, never underestimate the influence your work can have. Whether it's through the striking character you designed for a video game, the detailed model used in a high-budget film, or a personal project that resonates with others online, your art can inspire, inform, and entertain.

The beauty of digital sculpting is that it allows for the exploration of countless ideas without the limitations of traditional media. The freedom to experiment and iterate quickly is a unique advantage that enables you to explore complex ideas in a way that was once unimaginable.

Conclusion: A Journey That Never Ends

As you continue your digital sculpting journey, remember that this craft is always evolving. The techniques, tools, and processes you've learned here serve as a foundation, but they are by no means the final destination. Your growth as an artist will be shaped by how you continue to learn, adapt, and experiment.

Mastery comes with time, and even the most seasoned digital sculptors continue to explore new techniques, refine their craft, and push their creative boundaries. There will always be something new to learn, whether it's an advanced technique, a software update, or an entirely new medium to experiment with.

The most important thing is to never stop creating. Every new project, whether successful or challenging, is an opportunity to learn and grow. Let your passion for digital sculpting drive you forward, and remember that the skills and knowledge you've gained in this book are just the starting points for an exciting, ongoing journey. Your future in digital sculpting holds endless possibilities, and the best part is, you are the one in control of where it leads.

Appendices

The following appendices are designed to provide quick reference materials, tools, and resources to support your journey as a digital sculptor. Whether you're looking for specific brush settings, essential plugins, or additional learning resources, this section compiles everything you need to optimize your workflow, streamline your projects, and continue improving your craft. Each of the following appendices has been crafted with the intention of simplifying your creative process and expanding your knowledge base.

Brush Settings Cheat Sheets

When it comes to digital sculpting, your brushes are your primary tools. Understanding how to set up and use brushes effectively is essential to achieving your desired results. Below is a breakdown of common brush settings used in popular digital sculpting software, designed to optimize your workflow and give you better control over your creative process.

Standard Brush Settings

- **Intensity/Strength:** Controls the force with which the brush applies sculpting action. A higher intensity results in stronger deformation, while a lower setting allows for more subtle adjustments.

- **Size:** Determines the brush diameter. Larger sizes are useful for broad strokes, while smaller sizes provide finer, more detailed work.

- **Falloff:** Affects how the brush fades as it moves away from the center. A smooth falloff creates more gradual transitions, while sharp falloffs result in more defined edges.

- **Alpha:** Customizable shapes that determine the texture of the brush. Experiment with different alphas to achieve a variety of surface effects, from rough textures to intricate details.

- **Lazy Mouse:** A feature that helps create smoother, more controlled strokes by temporarily "lagging" the brush's path to reduce jitter.

Detail and Surface Brushes

- **Dam Standard:** Used for creating deep creases and sharp, angular lines. It's perfect for detailing hard surface models or creating intricate folds.

- **Clay Buildup:** Ideal for adding mass or volume to a model. This brush has a rougher, more textured application, making it ideal for creating organic forms like muscles or skin.

- **Smooth:** A must-have for smoothing over areas without affecting surrounding details. By adjusting the strength, you can create subtle smoothing or heavy smoothing for larger, rougher areas.

- **Pinch:** This brush pulls vertices together, making it useful for creating sharp details, such as seams or folds, by pinching two surfaces together.

Specialized Brushes

- **Trim Dynamic:** Perfect for hard-surface modeling, this brush flattens surfaces while maintaining sharp edges, useful for creating mechanical details.

- **HPolish:** A brush used to create polished, shiny surfaces. Ideal for refining smooth, hard-edged shapes.

- **Inflate:** This brush inflates or deflates the surface of a model, helping to add volume or subtract mass in areas where you need more subtle changes.

Tip: Always experiment with the pressure settings in combination with brush strength. This allows you to vary the intensity dynamically as you work, giving you more precision in each stroke.

Essential Plugins and Hotkeys Guide

To enhance your productivity and unlock more advanced capabilities, plugins and hotkeys are indispensable tools in your digital sculpting toolkit. Here is a collection of essential plugins and recommended hotkeys to help streamline your workflow.

Recommended Plugins

- **ZBrush to Photoshop (ZAppLink):** This plugin allows you to seamlessly send your model from ZBrush to Photoshop, where you can make texture or material adjustments, and then return the changes back to ZBrush without losing any detail. It's invaluable for texture painting and refining detail.

- **Decimation Master:** This plugin is a lifesaver when working with high-poly models. It reduces polygon count while maintaining as much detail as possible, ensuring your models are optimized for rendering or export.

- **NanoMesh:** NanoMesh allows you to use smaller objects or details that tile across a surface, providing great flexibility in detailing and texturing. It's perfect for creating intricate patterns or surface details on large objects.

- **Polygroup Master:** Used to organize your model into easy-to-select polygroups, this plugin simplifies the process of isolating areas for different types of work, such as detailing or UV unwrapping.

Must-Have Hotkeys

Hotkeys are shortcuts that help you work faster by giving you direct access to tools and actions. Here's a guide to some of the most useful hotkeys in digital sculpting:

- **S:** Toggle brush size quickly. Hold the hotkey and drag the mouse to adjust the brush size on the fly.

- **Shift:** While sculpting, holding Shift smooths the surface of your model. This is extremely useful for cleaning up rough spots.

- **Ctrl:** Inverts most brush actions, including selection and masking, allowing for quick reversals of any sculpting action.

- **Alt:** Inverts the effect of your brush (e.g., turning a standard brush into a "negative" effect). This is particularly useful for erasing or adding surface detail.

- **F:** Frame your model so that it fills the view, ensuring you're always centered on your work.

- **X:** Toggles symmetry, which is crucial for models that need to remain consistent on both sides.

- **Shift + F:** Toggles polyframe, allowing you to quickly view polygonal structure on your model.

These hotkeys can vastly reduce the time spent navigating through menus, allowing you to focus more on the creative process and less on technicalities.

Workflow Diagrams for Quick Reference

Sometimes, having visual aids can help simplify complex workflows, making them easier to follow and apply. The following workflow diagrams outline key sculpting processes, from the initial creation of a base mesh to finalizing details for a polished model.

Basic Sculpting Workflow

1. **Start with a Base Mesh:** Create a simple geometric form to begin sculpting. This mesh acts as the foundation for the model and can be shaped further.

2. **Block Out Major Forms:** Using broad strokes, establish the major shapes of the model. Focus on silhouette and proportion at this stage.

3. **Refine the Geometry:** After the basic forms are in place, start adding more refined details. Use tools like the Clay Buildup brush for volume and the Smooth brush for refining.

4. **Add Fine Details:** Use detailing brushes (e.g., Dam Standard or Pinch) to carve out smaller, intricate details.

5. **Polish and Smooth:** Once all the details are added, polish the surfaces with the HPolish or Smooth brush to refine the look and remove imperfections.

6. **Final Checks:** Review the model from multiple angles to ensure consistency and proportionality. Export it for texturing and rendering.

Texturing and Detailing Workflow

1. **UV Unwrapping:** Before applying textures, ensure the model's UVs are correctly laid out for efficient texturing. Use the UV Master plugin in ZBrush for automatic unwrapping.

2. **Base Texture Painting:** Using polygroups, apply base colors and textures using the Polygroups or Texture Map features in ZBrush.

3. **Add Surface Details:** Use a combination of alphas and custom brushes to add fine details such as skin pores, wrinkles, or hard-surface elements.

4. **Baking and Exporting:** Use tools like the ZBrush's "BPR" to bake details, which are then exported into your texturing program.

Recommended Resources (Courses, Mentorships, Communities)

Continuous learning and engaging with the digital sculpting community is essential for growth. Below are some valuable resources that will help you stay ahead of the curve and continue to improve your skills.

Online Courses

- **Gnomon:** Known for its high-quality courses in digital sculpting and 3D modeling, Gnomon offers in-depth learning materials for both beginners and advanced artists.

- **CGMA:** CGMA offers a wide range of specialized courses, including courses on character modeling, hard surface design, and texturing, all taught by professionals in the industry.

- **Udemy:** For more accessible courses, Udemy provides affordable options, including sculpting fundamentals and detailed workflow processes in popular digital sculpting software.

Mentorship Programs

- **ArtStation Mentorship Program:** A well-known platform that connects experienced artists with emerging talents. This mentorship program provides personalized guidance and feedback.

- **MasterClass:** MasterClass offers specialized courses from world-class artists and professionals in the field of digital art, including sculpting and 3D modeling.

Communities and Forums

- **ArtStation:** One of the most active and respected platforms for digital artists. Engaging with the community here can expose you to a wide range of techniques and opportunities.

- **ZBrushCentral:** The official community for ZBrush users, where you can find tutorials, tips, and support from other digital sculptors.

- **Polycount:** A forum that focuses on 3D art and game development. It's a great place to get feedback, learn new techniques, and stay updated on industry trends.

By utilizing these resources, you can continue refining your skills, connecting with others in the industry, and ensuring you remain competitive in the ever-evolving field of digital sculpting.

Frequently Asked Questions

Digital sculpting—especially at an advanced or professional level—can present an overwhelming range of techniques, tools, and production scenarios. Artists often encounter repeating uncertainties as they transition from intermediate practices to studio-level execution. This chapter addresses the most commonly asked questions related to sculpting workflow, tool configurations, output pipelines, and problem-solving strategies in ZBrush, providing clear, factual, and actionable guidance.

What Is the Ideal Polycount for Sculpting High-Resolution Detail?

The appropriate polygon count depends on the level of detail you're aiming for, the hardware you're working with, and how many subtools are active.

- For micro-pore skin sculpting or intricate surface etching, a typical subtool may require 10–20 million polygons.

- For primary and secondary forms, 1–2 million polygons per subtool is generally sufficient.

- Subtools should be subdivided individually. Avoid overloading a scene by subdividing everything uniformly.

To optimize performance:

- Use **DynaMesh** or **ZRemesher** to regulate polygon density during early form development.

- In the final detailing stage, isolate subtools and hide inactive ones to prevent memory strain.

How Do I Avoid Smoothing Out My Details When Subdividing?

Unintended smoothing during subdivision typically results from topology irregularities or inappropriate mesh resolution before increasing subdivision levels.

Recommendations:

- Before subdivision, use **ZRemesher** to even out the topology.

- Avoid subdividing low-resolution meshes that lack surface information. Add a mid-level of subdivision manually using **Divide**, then refine before proceeding further.

- Store a Morph Target before smoothing and use the **Morph Brush** to reintroduce original detail locally if necessary.

The best practice is to subdivide in controlled increments and constantly monitor how your detail evolves across levels.

How Do I Get Clean, Sharp Edges Without Using Hard Surface Techniques?

Sharp edges on organic models can be difficult to maintain with traditional brushes alone. A few techniques address this:

- Use **DamStandard** or **TrimDynamic** with lower focal shift for slicing in clean creases.

- **Pinch Brush** can tighten edges after they're defined, but should be used sparingly to avoid stretching topology.

- Build form around key shapes using **Move Topological** or **Move AccuCurve**, then cut sharper transitions with customized alphas.

- For ultimate edge fidelity, consider using **ZModeler** on isolated poly groups and integrate results with the sculpt.

Combining brush-based and geometry-based workflows often produces the cleanest sculptural results.

What's the Difference Between ZRemesher and DynaMesh?

Although both tools are used to manage mesh topology, they serve distinct purposes.

- **DynaMesh** is best used during the blocking phase. It redistributes polygons evenly based on mesh volume and resolution settings. It supports additive sculpting but destroys subdivision levels.

- **ZRemesher** creates more predictable edge loops and quadrangle-dominated topology ideal for animation or projection. It preserves form better than DynaMesh and allows controlled retopology using guides and symmetry settings.

Use DynaMesh to explore form, and switch to ZRemesher when preparing for detail sculpting or export.

How Can I Rebuild Subdivision Levels After Retopology?

If you've retopologized a mesh outside ZBrush or lost subdivision levels during sculpting, you can reproject your high-resolution details onto a subdividable mesh.

Steps:

1. Subdivide your new mesh gradually until the polygon count roughly matches the original high-res sculpt.

2. Use **SubTool > Project All** at each level to transfer detail.

3. Repeat projection at each subdivision level until you've restored all surface information.

Always compare side-by-side during projection. Adjust **Dist** (distance) and use the **Project Brush** for manual corrections.

How Do I Fix Pinching or Stretching at Joints?

Pinching around elbows, knees, and fingers often results from low-density or uneven topology.

Solutions include:

- Use **ZRemesher** with guides to redirect edge flow around problematic joints.

- Manually add edge loops or increase resolution before subdividing if you're using **ZModeler**.

- Avoid overusing the **Inflate** or **Move** brushes in joint areas without smoothing transitions afterward.

Evaluate deformation under posing scenarios by using **Transpose Master** to preview whether skin and forms compress and extend properly.

What's the Best Workflow for Sculpting a Full Character?

An efficient full-character workflow depends on the desired output: animation, concept sculpt, or 3D print. A common sculpting pipeline includes:

1. **ZSpheres or Base Mesh**: Establish the form or pose.

2. **DynaMesh**: Block out mass, anatomy, and large forms.

3. **ZRemesher**: Create manageable topology and prepare for clean subdivision.

4. **Subdivision and Projection**: Add detail progressively through subdivision levels.

5. **Polypaint or Texturing**: Apply vertex color or prepare UVs and bake maps.

6. **Export**: Generate displacement, normal, and texture maps.

Splitting the model into multiple subtools (head, limbs, clothing, etc.) ensures that each part receives appropriate attention without sacrificing performance.

Can I Use ZBrush for Game-Ready Asset Production?

Yes. While ZBrush focuses on high-resolution sculpting, it plays a critical role in game asset creation:

- Sculpt the high-resolution detail in ZBrush.

- Retopologize using **ZRemesher** or export to other applications (e.g., Maya, Blender, or TopoGun).

- Unwrap UVs in ZBrush using **UV Master** or externally.

- Bake maps (normal, displacement, AO) inside ZBrush or with third-party tools (e.g., Marmoset Toolbag, Substance 3D).

- Export the low-resolution game mesh along with baked textures.

ZBrush is most effective in the high-poly phase and as part of a broader toolchain that includes real-time renderers.

How Do I Improve My Sculpting Brush Control?

Brush control comes from both tool familiarity and hardware optimization.

Suggestions:

- Use a high-resolution drawing tablet with pressure sensitivity. Tablets with tilt support add even more nuance.

- Modify **Brush > Curve > Focal Shift and Falloff** settings to fine-tune stroke behavior.

- Customize Lazy Mouse settings for smoother, more deliberate strokes.

- Practice stroke tapering and surface transitions on anatomical studies or simple primitive shapes.

Consistent repetition under varying forms and materials trains your eye and hand to work in synergy.

Why Does My Polypaint Look Pixelated?

Polypaint depends on vertex color, not texture maps. Low-resolution meshes have fewer vertices, which limits the amount of color detail you can apply.

Fixes include:

- Subdivide the mesh before painting. Each subdivision increases color fidelity.

- For texture-based painting, unwrap the model and export UVs before baking the polypaint to texture.

- Consider using **HD Geometry** if your hardware allows it, enabling fine-level painting without excessive subtool subdivision.

Polypaint is ideal for sculpting-phase color planning, while UV-based painting serves final texturing needs.

When Should I Use HD Geometry?

HD Geometry is designed for ultra-fine detailing—beyond 20–30 million polygons per subtool. It allows subdivision beyond the regular maximum while keeping the rest of the model in standard resolution.

Use it for:

- Pores, wrinkles, and skin microfolds.

- Engraved patterns or extreme displacement needs.

- Museum-level or cinematic close-up assets.

HD Geometry is not compatible with some export or render functions (e.g., map baking), so plan its use for specific stages rather than general sculpting.

How Do I Export a Model with Polypaint and Displacement Maps?

To export both color and surface detail:

1. Ensure your model has clean UVs.

2. Use **Multi Map Exporter** to generate Displacement, Normal, and Color maps.

3. Choose TIFF or EXR for high-bit-depth maps.

4. Set scale, flip options, and subtool selections carefully.

Export your mesh as OBJ or FBX and include texture maps. Use a consistent naming structure to avoid mismatches during import into rendering or game engines.

What Causes Crashing When Working with Large Projects?

Crashes usually result from exceeding RAM limits, GPU overload, or corrupt subtools.

Preventative tips:

- Keep subtools under 20–30 million polygons where possible.

- Save incrementally and enable **QuickSave**.

- Optimize subtool use—merge only when necessary.

- Disable shadows, perspective, or matcap previews temporarily when managing heavy scenes.

- If corruption is suspected, duplicate and export subtools separately, then reassemble in a fresh ZBrush project.

Regular performance monitoring and file hygiene extend stability in high-demand projects.

How Do I Prepare a Model for 3D Printing?

ZBrush includes tools specifically geared toward preparing models for additive manufacturing.

Steps include:

1. Ensure mesh is **watertight** using **Close Holes** or **Live Boolean** merges.

2. Use **DynaMesh** to merge intersecting parts into solid volume.

3. Apply **Decimation Master** to reduce file size while retaining detail.

4. Export using **3D Print Hub** and set scale in millimeters.

5. Choose **STL** or **OBJ** for compatibility with slicer software.

Print prep also includes slicing and hollowing, which can be done either in ZBrush or external tools like Meshmixer.

Is There a Correct Way to Store and Organize Brushes?

Yes. Proper organization saves time and promotes consistency:

- Save custom brushes using **Brush > Save As** into a designated folder under **ZStartup/BrushPresets**.

- Group brushes by category (e.g., "Organic," "Trim," "Hard Surface").

- Use naming conventions that reflect purpose and pressure behavior (e.g., "SkinDetail_LowPress.ZBP").

Back up brush libraries externally and sync them across workstations if working in a shared studio environment.

www.ingramcontent.com/pod-product-compliance
Lightning Source LLC
LaVergne TN
LVHW060139070326

832902LV00018B/2866